The Slayer Codex VOL2

Unearthing Vampires:
Identify and remove energy
vampires from your life once and
for all

Author: Michelle T Holland

Unearthing Vampires: The Slayer Codex Volume 2
Copyright © 2017 Michelle T. Holland
All Rights Reserved
Published by Michelle T. Holland

This book is a work of fiction. Names, characters, places and incidents are products of the author's imagination or are used fictitiously. The use of artist, song titles, famous people, book titles, locations and products throughout this book are done for storytelling purposes and are in no way to be seen as an advertisement. Trademark names are used in an editorial fashion, with no intention of infringement of the respective owner's trademark.

National Library of Australia Cataloguing-in-Publication Data available.

ISBN 978-0-6480066-3-3 (Paperback)
ISBN 978-0-6480066-2-6 (eBook)

Cover Designed by: ETI Image
Illustrations by: Joel Villamil

www.michelletholland.com

Table of Contents

Dedication:

To my strong female friends who provide me with the support and love that I need to become the kind of vampire slayer that I want to be. You know who you are and you are awesome!

Part 1: Unearthing Vampires

There are darknesses in life and there are lights, and you are one of the lights, the light of all lights."
— Bram Stoker, Dracula

Michelle T Holland

Chapter 1: So Not a Fairy-tale

*All the adversity I've had in my life,
all my troubles and obstacles, have
strengthened me... You may not
realize it when it happens, but a kick
in the teeth may be the best thing in
the world for you. - Walt Disney*

Once upon a time there was a young girl. She was happy, successful and loved her life. She grew up, faced a big problem and nasty demon. She slayed the demon, fixed the problem, and lived happily ever after. The End.

Have you ever noticed that life never behaves like in a fairytale?

I don't know about you, but I grew up watching Wonder Woman and Buffy the Vampire Slayer instead of Disney Princess movies. I'm glad I had this start in life because it's helped me to become the person that I was supposed to be. The stories in Wonder Woman were not fairy tales. Buffy didn't get her Prince and 'happily ever after'. And that's life.

Like many young girls I wanted to have a beautiful, adventurous and love filled life. I I listened to regular society this meant that I had to find a man, get married, get a good job, buy a house, work hard to pay bills, have children, live for a bit more travelling and paying bills and then…die.

That's the story that most of us are fed throughout our lives. This story comes from all of the well-meaning people in our life. It is a story provided with love, tenderness and compassion. It's a story that is told over and over again. This story is the fairytale, and sets us up for disappointment.

Wonder Woman was a warrior princess and although the TV version had her subordinated to a male at work, it was clear that this wasn't who she was. When you read the comics it shows a much stronger character than the TV would lead us to believe. It was the 70s though, and feminism was still something that was 'done to men' rather than something that allows all people to be equal. They are about to release a new Wonder Women movie and from the looks of the movie trailer, WW has found her place in kick ass girl history.

I loved WW but there was still something missing for me. When I found Buffy, I found what I was missing, because Buffy was different. Buffy was a girl who loved fashion, shoes, boys, having fun with her friends, watching TV with her mom, and eating "more sugar than the human body can stand". She was a normal girl, except that on a regular basis she also fought the forces of darkness and saved the world.

The thing that made Buffy resonate with me, and many other young people, was that Buffy's life was not a fairytale. The pain that she dealt with through broken hearts, broken friendships, school bullying and disappointment with the adults in her life, was real and relatable. I mean she saved the world, but she didn't get a big happy ending. Her friends died and she certainly didn't ride off with anyone tall, dark or handsome. Instead she rode off with a group of young scared women who needed her leadership.

So the question that continued to pop into my mind throughout my love affair with this show, and since, is why is the 'fairytale' still the thing we strive for?

Why do we think that we just have to get through this one next thing and love will be waiting for us? A big strong man will sweep us off our feet and carry us into the sunset. It seems so unreal and very unlikely, and yet this fairytale prevails in the stories we tell our young girls.

You can watch any movie, TV show or book that is aimed at young women and there is always a tall, gorgeous love interest that sweeps them off their feet. Alternatively, the tall, gorgeous love interest breaks their heart and they spend the next episode or half the movie pinning for the guy.

The Twilight books and movies are a good example of this. Essentially the story goes, sad quiet mousy girl meets gorgeous brooding guy, he shows her his flaws, she falls in love, he breaks her heart sending her into the arms of someone else, she becomes more sad, then the guy comes back, tells her that he loves her and she blossoms and becomes beautiful.

Sigh. Don't get me wrong. I read and watched the movies, and I liked them for entertainment value. What concerns me is that we constantly replay the Romeo and Juliet story over and over again. Girl meets boy, girl loses herself in boy, and can't live without him.

Buffy, yep she met a tall brooding guy, and yep he left and broke her heart, but did she wait for him to come back and save her? Nope. She just got on with the job of saving the world. She mended her broken heart through making mistakes, asking her mentors for help, and going the Bronze with her friends.

She was a girl, she behaved like a girl, and she was a leader, and behaved like a leader. This showed me as a young girl that you could be both. You can be a leader, you can save the world, and you can still be a girl in killer heels. It says that you can have your heart broken, you can love, and you can still kick ass.

The fairytale is a myth and the sooner we all woman up and realise that the better.

I'm not telling you this as some big female power statement, and this is not a book about feminism, so fella's you are safe to continual reading. The reason I am reflecting on these lessons is to tell you its not too late to change your thinking about the dreams, myths, and stories that were fed to you by the well-meaning people in your life.

Maybe they told you that you couldn't be creative and earn money. Perhaps you were told that being a soccer player was only something you do on the weekend. You may have heard 'its ok to be gay around us honey, but the world won't understand, so stay quiet'. Maybe you were told that 97% of all small business fail, so save yourself the pain. You may have been told that you could be an engineer, but prepare yourself because it's really hard for a girl to get a job fixing airplanes.

Any time you seek to have something that is outside of what is seen as right and proper, AKA normal. You will be faced with people telling you that you can't or you mustn't. They don't understand that you have a strength that they haven't tapped into yet. They don't understand that for you to be an accountant instead of a photographer will eat away at your soul. They don't understand it, because a well meaning person helped them when they were young to avoid the pain of following their dream.

These well meaning people tell you these things because they think they are protecting you from the hard realities of life. They want to protect you like the well meaning person protected them when they were young. They don't know that they are setting you up for a life that you will continually struggle with. They don't understand that this isn't who you are and that by keeping you from your dream allows the vampire inside to creep in and take over.

Oh, by the way, did I mention that I'm a Vampire Slayer?

You might already know this about me because I'm hoping that you have read volume one of The Slayer Codex. If you have read it then you are primed and ready to take on the vampires of the world. You are two steps ahead and will unearth these vamps with a click of your fingers.

If you haven't read the first volume then I suggest you buy, beg, borrow or steal it (actually don't steal it), and read it when you can. I'll give you a quick recap on it here, but it won't do it justice because the best part about volume one is that is helps you to become a Vampire Slayer.

Here's my quick and dirty recap.

I discovered that I was a Vampire Slayer after a particularly long time of working in a very toxic work environment. This workplace, that I affectionately call "Hades", was not unlike many workplaces. It had lots of people, doing lots of work. It had experienced people, and inexperienced people. It had a culture that included people keeping their heads down so they didn't get in trouble and had people at the top dictating the way in which everyone was to work and behave. It also had a major infestation of vampires.

They were in the boardroom, the executive office, the clerical pool, the interns, the long-terms, and throughout middle management.

They were everywhere.

Many workplaces have vampires. If you are already in the workforce you'll be reading this going, no shit! If you are about to enter the workforce, prepare yourself because the vampires that you went to school with, that annoyed you in college, are in the workplace too. The vampires are usually contained to a small area if there is strong management at the top, however at 'Hades' management were all vampires. They had taken on the vampire persona with a flair that I've only ever seen in the movies. Consequently, my Slayer felt very out of place and was treated badly.

I didn't know that 'Hades' was infested with vamps before I accepted the job. I would have run the other way if I'd know what it was like. My Guru Harry did know, and he let me leave his business to go work there.

I was angry at Harry when I first found out that he had let me go to this horrible place without telling me that the vampires would try and consume me while I was there. My anger soon became understanding when he explained that he hadn't said anything to me because he knew that I'd learn more at 'Hades' about vampires and how to slay them than him telling me.

Although I had other teachers in my life, Harry was my first formal Slayer Guru. He told me about the vampires and he taught me a number of lessons that I used to survive at 'Hades'. When I look back on my time at 'Hades' I know I wouldn't have made it out alive without the preparation and lessons that Harry gave me.

Once I left 'Hades' I freelanced for a few years, working extremely hard. I was determined to eradicate the world of vampires. I was determined to be the one that saved the world. Like Buffy I always did it in killer heels. Acting more like Bella from Twilight, I didn't draw on support when I needed it so I came crashing down hard. I had ignored the warning signals that were going off in my head telling me that I was about to burn out. That's when I experienced my "Homer Simpson Nuclear Meltdown" and had to change the way I was looking and experiencing life. I won't go into it now, you can read about it in volume one, but its fair to say that I wasn't in a fit state and only a big change in the way I lived my life was going to help me.

Once I pulled myself through, I developed the SLAYER methodology.

The SLAYER methodology is an ensemble of the knowledge and lessons that I have accumulated over many years of slaying. Through trial and error I have established a system that worked for me, and has worked for many of the up and coming Slayers that I continue to grow and mentor.

The system of the Slayer won't work for everyone. Not because it's not suitable for everyone, its just it's a pretty full on commitment and many people aren't ready for that commitment. The system takes you through six key elements that provide a guide for strengthening your inner power and releasing your Slayer. Once the Slayer is released, the methodology helps you strengthen her.

You see we all have a vampire living within, and without a strong Slayer we can become susceptible to the toxin of the vampire. The vampire can show up in your life at the most inopportune moments. He regularly pops up when you are feeling vulnerable, hurt or scared. How successful your vampire is from distracting you away from your purpose is all to do with the strength of your Slayer.

Your Slayer's job is to take care of business and remove the influence of the vampire. There are many ways in which your Slayer can do this, however the most effective way is keeping you connected to your purpose and your mission.

I told you I was a Slayer. I still have a vampire and a human, but I identify myself as a Slayer because that is the part of me that I engage with the most. My human is always there and I find her regularly when I'm engaged in a loving relationship, or watching a PETA commercial. She is the compassionate side of me. My vampire is one seriously pissed off bloodsucker. This is because I don't allow him to take hold of me. When he does pop in for a visit, it's an epic battle of wills and he comes at me with a vengeance. This is not unusual when you strengthen your Slayer. Your vamp really wants to bring her down a peg or two.

If this is the first time you have been introduced to the concept of the vampire, the Slayer and the human then I urge you to read volume one. In that volume I tell you about my transition to becoming a Slayer. You see I was born human and I grew up human. I was just a normal girl and grew up in a very normal way. It wasn't until I was in my 20s that I really discovered that I was a Slayer and that I could do the most amazing things when I allowed my Slayer to step forward and lead. It was also at that time that I discovered that my vampire, and the vampires of others, can be extremely strong and I need to be constantly vigilant.

Throughout this transition I had the support of a marvellous Guru called Harry. Harry helped me to understand what it means to be a Slayer, and how to keep her strong. He also helped me to identify and slay vampires. Internal vampires are often the toughest to deal with, but you will come across vampires external to yourself also. These vampires come in various forms. Some are stronger than others, and some have a greater personal impact than others.

Most people that you meet are human. I will tell you how to recognize a human as opposed to a vampire or a Slayer later on but I want to draw your attention to the fact that the vast majority of people are human. They make mistakes of course, but they remain human. They can take the lead and take risks, but they remain human. Thankfully this is the way of life, because a world full of Slayers and vampires would be a turbulent place indeed. The human provides the balance.

Ultimately integration is the goal. You won't eradicate the vampires completely from your life, and nor should you. There is a beautiful verse in the Tao Te Ching that explains to us that we must have the darkness to be able to enjoy the light. We must experience bad to recognise the good. One of my favourite sections of this 2500 year old text tells us that if we experience terrible things its only because we have experienced the opposite. We know hunger because we have felt full. We feel sadness only because we have felt happy. These verses help me to accept the vampire.

The vampires that we encounter as we walk through our lives help us to see the beauty and the strength that we can have. I have been so weak I just wanted to close my eyes and never open them again. But I opened them because I had been strong previously and I knew I could again. This is the essence of the Slayer methodology, to integrate the three selves, ie: the human, the Slayer and the vampire.

Unearthing Vampires

When many people first start on this journey, including me, they try to eradicate the vampire entirely which just results in a very annoyed vamp who fights for survival. When the vamp is in a fight for survival your Slayer is distracted and the human has to fend for themself. Let me give you an example to explain.

Carl contacted me after reading an earlier version of The Slayer Codex. When I met Carl I had been full Slayer for a number of years. I was in a position of strength and health. I started to work with Carl because he decided that he wanted change. He knew that something was missing from his life and he want to connect with his bigger mission. Carl followed the Slayer methodology to the letter, and he was worked hard to strengthen his Slayer. Carl saw me as his Guru, which of course was flattering; unfortunately his vampire decided that a great way of distracting Carl away from his mission was to start comparing himself with me.

It's a quick pathway to disappointment, anxiety and depression when you start to compare yourself to someone who is on a very different path to you. To compare your beginning to someone's middle is to prime the environment for the vampire.

This is exactly what Carl started to do. He felt that he was working hard and should have eradicated his vampire. I touched base with Carl after being away for a month and found him unable to enjoy life because a darkness had begun to set in. After a big talk and a lot of tears, I discovered that Carl was beating himself up because his vampire kept popping up to say hello. He was desperate to become a musician but every time he had time to play his guitar, he couldn't focus and instead reached for the remote and started watching Reality TV while sitting on the couch eating Doritos. Each time he would berate himself for being lazy and not engaging with his music. He told himself that he wasn't a good musician anyway and no-one wanted to hear his music. Then he would question his commitment to becoming a Slayer because he knew that this nasty inner voice was his vampire. He couldn't get rid of this voice and he thought that he'd failed as a Slayer.

"The only failure is in giving up." I said to him that day. This was something that Harry had taught to me and I had found out myself. Failure is not a problem; in fact it's an essential part of life. Every time you fail and allow the vampire to pop in for a cappuccino is an opportunity to strengthen your Slayer. Your Slayer will become better and better at ridding the vampire from your life, but its never eradicated. Once I explained to Carl that his vampire will always be with him and will constantly test him, he felt relieved. He thought because I was so strong that I had eradicated my vampire. I assured him that my vamp paid me a visit from time to time just to make sure I was still committed to my mission.

It's easy to think that we want to get rid of the bad things in our life for good, but on the contrary these are the things that show us the amazing life we have.

Instead of spending all of your time and effort in beating down the vampire, and then beating yourself up for allowing the vampire to surface, thank him. Thank the vampire inside, and the vampires you meet in life for coming into your life. It is through their darkness that you can discover and enjoy your light.

Chapter 2: Let's Do This

> **Each experience in your life was absolutely necessary in order to have gotten you to the next place, and the next place, up to this very moment. — Wayne W. Dyer**

I'm going to start by giving you a quick recap on the Slayer methodology. But first I want to remind you that although I want you to read, digest and love the methodology, its not for everyone and what I'd like to do is instead invite you to read and consider the methodology.

My goal is not to convince you that you will be better off with a strong Slayer and a life of meaning and purpose. That is true for me, and true for many people I've worked with, but it may not be true for you. A better outcome for me is that you consider the words and the principles that are provided in the methodology and that this consideration sets you on a pathway that is right for you.

There were many books and methodologies that I picked up throughout my life that I put down again because they weren't right for me. I read, considered, cherry picked the bit I liked and then moved on. At times what I picked up wasn't right for me at all at the time, and yet years later I gobbled it up with a hunger that it couldn't satisfy the first time. A good example of this is the book called "Eat, Pray, Love". I'm sure you've heard of this book. If not and you were living in a cave for the past 10 years I'll explain.

"Eat, Pray, Love" is the memoirs of author Elizabeth Gilbert from a particularly enlightening time in her life. She had gone through excruciating pain and loss without the skills for dealing with it. Her vampire was in full force. She decided that she needed change and needed to connect to a bigger purpose and her bigger mission. She left her home for a year to go on a journey to experience, pleasure and spiritual connectedness, and to find balance between the two.

When I first read this book I wasn't in a position to enjoy it. I couldn't connect with her pain, and I didn't share her need for spiritual arousal. In fact, her story kind of annoyed my young self and therefore I put it down half finished. Fast forward ten years and I was post my traumatic 'Hades' and 'Homer' experiences and I started to read Gilbert's memoirs again. I can't even remember why I picked it up again but for some reason it called to me. This time I read every chapter and hung on every word. Her pain was real for me, and her spiritual journey not unlike my own. Well, she spent 8 months in India and Bali meditating while I spent that time slaying vampires, but you know what they say in Thailand…same, same but different.

Her story hadn't changed, but I had and therefore I was ready to accept the teachings into my life. This is why I won't tell you that you are a twit if you don't get the Slayer methodology or you don't like it, or you think it's trite. Instead I just say thank you for taking the time to taste something different and perhaps later on it will be more flavoursome for you.

The thing I know to be true, is if I hadn't read some of "Eat, Pray, Love" when I did I would be missing a piece of the puzzle that would eventually lead me back to the book.

Below is a short, sharp and shiny version of the methodology. If you have read volume one recently then by all means skip ahead, if it's been a while then have a read and remind yourself of the principles.

The Method

The Slayer Methodology Refresh

Element 1: Self-Full

Self-full is looking after yourself, filling your own cup first, acknowledging that you must be full and healthy before you can take action to help others. Self-full is recognising that your mind and your body perform best

Michelle T Holland

when you are providing it with the rest, nourishment, and mindful activity it needs.

- Key 1: Social Connection - We are essentially social creatures by nature. We feel safe when there are people around us to defend and fend for us.
- Key 2: Enjoyment - Enjoyment is something that you love to do, just because you love to do it.
- Key 3: Live Creatively - Living creatively will enable you to have the kind of resilience that comes from a full cup.
- Key 4: Me Time - Taking time for you enables you to give more freely to others.
- Key 5: Healthy Habits - You have to focus on your health and wellbeing, or it will let you down.
- Key 6: Future Focus - To really achieve meaning in your life, and help others achieve meaning in theirs, have a clear vision of your ideal future.

Element 2: Learning

You learn for passion, you learn for pleasure AND you take deliberate action to be current and learn every day...on purpose. You challenge your beliefs and stretch your knowledge to think like a leader. You learn from every opportunity and you push yourself to think beyond your current ideas and ideals.

- Key 1: Focused and Purposeful Learning - Learning is strategic and supports the outcomes of your current goals while supporting the achievement of your future vision.
- Key 2: Strategic Thinking and Learning - A plan of action that ensures that you keep the big picture in mind.

- Key 3: Curiosity Equals Knowledge - Curiosity begets knowledge, and knowledge keeps you safe.
- Key 4: Read, Read, Read, Listen - The most successful people in the world read. They read a lot and they read often.
- Key 5: Finding a Guru - Proximity psychology states that you become the average the people that you spend the most time with.
- Key 6: Success Through Experiment - Be curious, and actively search out new experiences…its hard to go wrong.
- Key 7: Start to love the 'F' Word - Focus on compassion, kindness and helping someone grow and you will relish, not resist, feedback.

Element 3: Agile
You are flexible in your thinking and your behaviour. You believe that moving with change assists you to grow and you take action based on this belief. Emotional intelligence, resilience, leadership, relationships, work, and life…all require you to flex. A Slayer can flex, and sees the clear benefit of being flexible.

- Key 1: Life is Messy - Through discomfort comes the greatest learning. Allow yourself and others to feel the discomfort.
- Key 2: In Flexibility We Trust - Remove judgements about the people you work or live with, and having the strength of character to bend, but not break.
- Key 3: Agility Ability - Be unique, contribute your abilities and be careful of expecting others to contribute at the same level as you.

- Key 4: Momentum - For real change, use momentum to increase your time, energy and sustainability.

Element 4: Yogish

Yogish means knowing that everything you do affects someone or something. You think about the big stuff, you dream, you're curious AND you take deliberate action to cultivate these abilities. Every action has a consequence, and every behaviour is a choice. Your thinking can change your being, and vice versa. Your mind is powerful.

- Key 1: Vulnerability - The key to a heart filled journey into vulnerability, is the need to be connected to a bigger purpose.
- Key 2: Manifesting Your Ass Off - Put energy into the positive and people and circumstances will be more attracted to you.
- Key 3: Integration of Selves - It is a daily practice of understanding your role in the world and how you impact it and are impacted by it.
- Key 4: A Life of Meaning - A compelling vision will light a beacon in your heart and mind that the vampire can not bear.

Element 5: Entrepreneurial

You get stuff done, you set goals, you take deliberate action, you think strategically, and you enable others to follow you and contribute to your vision. To be a truly great leader you need to have a vision that others understand and care about creating with you. You have passion, drive, and energy, and you succeed without harm to yourself or others.

Unearthing Vampires

- Key 1: Don't Be a Vampire - Vampires are not entrepreneurial in the SLAYER framework.
- Key 2: Create a Compelling Vision - A compelling vision will keep you energised and focused.
- Key 3: Get Shit Done - Your dreams will stay dreams if you don't work hard at it. Rewards come through effort.
- Key 4: Welcome Failure - Failure is an opportunity to learn and grow. "The person who never made a mistake, never made anything."
- Key 5: Surprise the Crap Out of Yourself - Take calculated risk. Check your fears to see if they are unreasonable or reasonable. Flip your thinking. Take a risk. Achieve amazing things.
- Key 6: Be The Kind of Human That You Would Follow - "Just be human first." Focus first on the relationship, and secondly on the tasks that need completed. Be active in your humanness.

R – Relationships

Good relationships build you up and poor relationships can pull you down. Having amazing people in your corner can assist you to solve problems, be recommended for projects or promotion, they provide much needed support when the chips are down and they can simply improve your environment and conditions by providing a light-hearted release in an otherwise tough environment.

- Key 1: Understand Yourself - Relationships start and end with you. If you don't know who you are then how can you ever understand anyone else?

- Key 2: Respond to Diversity and Differences in Others - Speak in a language that they understand so that they hear you.
- Key 3: Picking Your Battles - Ask yourself before 'fighting', is that issue so important that you are willing to damage your relationship?
- Key 4: Sometimes Honesty is Enough - By communicating the truth, you stand a better chance of keeping your relationships intact.
- Key 5: Balancing Strength with Heart and Humanity - Love, compassion and empathy can shine a very bright light. Vampires hate the light.

On 'The Slayer Codex' website you can access some additional bonus resources that may help you to implement the keys at www.theSlayercodex.com/bookbonuses.

So that's how you strengthen your Slayer. Regular and daily actions and commitments to doing better today than you did yesterday. Success happens through action, not by accident.

Before we move onto the part where I introduce you to the vampires, let me take a moment to describe the Slayer.

YOU CAN BE THE LIGHT THAT
CONQUERS THE DARKNESS.

Michelle T Holland

Chapter 3: The Slayer

"Nothing can dim the light which shines from within." — *Maya Angelou.*

The easy answer to who is the slayer is to say, 'I am the Slayer'.

Hey, when you read that, can you add a Batman voice to it? *I am the Slayer...* sounds all official and stuff.

Any hoo, that's true. I am a slayer, and so are you, if you choose of course. In volume one I go into great detail about what the slayer is all about. But that's in a whole other book that you may or may not choose to read. I mean 300 odd pages of book isn't everyone cup of tea. No worries, totally get it. So here is the 50 cent version of what a slayer is. All you need really is that she is inside of you, just waiting for the day that you unleash her.

Let me tell you a little bit about the slayer.

Michelle T Holland

She is the strength within you. She is the part of you that remains quiet until the day when you need her. She steps up in the times of darkness, when you are struggling to see the light at the end of the tunnel. She is the part of you that sheds a light, when the tunnel appears completely darkened.

When you are scared and something inside of you says keep going, it's her voice you hear. When you think that you don't have the courage to have that conversation, dive off that diving board, or ask for that payrise, she gives you a gentle kick in the pants and you find the courage.

The voice in your head that tells you that you are good enough, that you can do it and you are worthy – that's her.

She is that part of you that drags you out off bed in the morning when all you want to do is pull the cover over your head and ignore the world. She is the one who marches up to that bully on the street to save the person being victimised. He is the one that speaks up at the meeting about the injustice that you have witnessed at work.

She is your strength.

She is your courage.

She is your wisdom.

She is your passion.

She embodies your purpose.

She keeps you safe, and protects you when you feel scared.

She is the light inside of you that shines so bright, that everyone around you envy your happiness and your passion. When you allow her to shine, she will light up the dark corners of your life.

Unearthing Vampires

The vampire that you have been dealing with your whole life hides away. She is you, and you are she. Once you accept your inner strength, the light that comes from within you shines so bright that the darkness has no choice but to fade away.

Your life and your success relies on you having the capability and skill to handle your vampire, and to recognise and slay the vampires in your world.

Just a quick side note, slay means to remove the vampires influence from your life, and at time when it comes to external vampires, to remove them completely from having any interaction with you. Removing toxic people and energy from your world is a good place to start your Slayer journey because you are making decisions about the kind of life that you want to live. If you want to live a life of meaning and purpose, you want to minimise the negative distractions as much as possible. Plus, unless you are going to go full Slayer and start slaying vampires for a living, you have your own vampire to deal with and that will keep your Slayer busy enough without having to deal with other people's vampires all the time. Slay quickly and decisively and you will make a shift towards your ultimate purpose.

Once you learn the secrets of the vampires and how to slay them its very hard to go back to being ignorant about the things that happen in the world. It becomes difficult to ignore poor behavior, difficult people, and toxic attitudes.

There are many more vampires than I've covered in this book. Many of the vampires you find in your life may only be vampires for a temporary period of time.

Although I provide a methodology that works in many cases, each and every vampire has their own unique qualities. There will be times that the vampire you find doesn't respond well to the methods. If you get to a point by which you have exhausted your Slayer kit bag and you can't slay or save, then call in an expert. This may be someone like me, or a highly trained specialist Slayer. I give you some hints about this in the section titled 'Van Helsing'.

So let's get started and learn how to identify the vampires.

Part 2: Recognise the Vampires

"Remember to always be yourself. Unless you suck."
— Joss Whedon

Michelle T Holland

Chapter 4: The Humans

Do I want to be a hero to my son? No. I would like to be a very real human being. That's hard enough. - Robert Downey,   Jr.

Generally humans are humans. I know that seems like a daft thing to say but I want to make sure that you recognise humans as well as vampires. When you start out on this journey the temptation is to see vampire behaviours in everyone where before you only saw the human.

So before we get started recognising vampires I want to talk to you about humans. You see the issue with humans is that we are beautifully and perfectly imperfect. Each of us has areas of improvement and each of us can display vampire behaviours at any time.

I was speaking with a Slayer buddy of mine the other night. She's having a particularly tough time at work at the moment. Her boss is a vampire. Normally this Slayer is extremely skilled at slaying and she identifies early and slays with grace. I'm very proud, she's one of my star pupils.

She spoke to me in length about the feelings of disappointment that she had in her inability to slay this vampire that she was dealing with. The vampire in question is particularly difficult to deal with because she flips from being an alpha to a minion without blinking. This is no surprise to me. There are particularly difficult vampires in the world. Ones that are very skilled at being a vampire because it has always worked for them. The interesting part of the conversation was the Slayer telling me that she thought that she was becoming a vampire.

She was quite distressed about this because she had always prided herself on her Slayer skills. Even when she

was human she display strong Slayer skills. So thinking that she was becoming a vampire was taking its toll on her.

As we discussed her predicament further it became evident that she was not becoming a vampire, but she was displaying vampire behaviours under certain conditions. Even others in the team had noticed and had told her that they saw the vampire behaviours when she was in specific situations. She found herself behaving like an alpha at times when dealing with the vampire and at other time flipping into minion behaviours. She was mimicking the behaviour of this vampire.

This is the destructive power of vampires in the office. Particularly those vampires that have made their way up the chain and appear to have the support of other alpha vampires. Their toxin is strong and can infect even the strongest of Slayers.

I tell you this story not to scare you because I know that this Slayer will either solve the problem of the vampire, or she will eventually leave the organisation because the vampire infestation may be too thick to fight. I know she will be fine and she will shake off the vampire toxin because that's the kind of Slayer she is. She's strong and resilient.

I tell you this story because you, as a new Slayer, may mistake this other Slayer as a vampire if you haven't been given the whole story or you haven't witness her other qualities.

Its important when on a Slayer journey to recognise that some behaviours in humans (and other Slayers for that matter) may be a symptom of the immediate environment and not a symptom of vampirism.

Michelle T Holland

You must seek to understand the whole situation and you must seek to look at the person within the context of their life and the working environment. This is a situation where you need to look beyond the walls they have put up, and see that the person is a Slayer displaying vampire traits in a particular situation and circumstances.

There's a danger is judging humans as vampires too soon. When you do that you can miss the real vampires in the office.

Identifying Humans:

- They make mistakes

- They are tolerant of others mistakes

- They sometimes display vampire behaviours in specific situations

- They act appropriately more often than they don't

- Other people comment on how out of character vampire behaviours are

- Other people and Slayers speak highly of the person

- They achieve great things for themselves and others

- They are loving and compassionate

- They are human

Remember that the human displaying vampire behaviours still needs to have these behaviours addressed and eradicated. There is no excuse for poor behaviours, but there are often reasons for it. So firstly discover the person beyond the situation and then understand the reasons for the behaviours, and then determine how to assist this person to shake off the toxins of the vampire that they are working with.

Chapter 5: The Alpha

Darkness cannot drive out darkness; only light can do that. Hate cannot drive out hate; only love can do that.
– Martin Luther King, Jr.

This chapter was hard for me to write. I put it off till near the end of the book knowing that I was going to have to relive the pain. It's difficult when I reflect on my failings in this area, my struggles, and my hardships. Yet I know that I need to do it because if I can save one person from this kind of vampire then it's worth the pain.

The Alpha is what I call them. You met Vincent already. He's an example of an alpha of the worst kind. What makes Vincent a real danger to you as an aspiring Slayer is he has the ability to charm and deceive quickly and easily. He has the ability to convert people to become vampires themselves. He has so much power that one Slayer alone doesn't cut it.

Remember my experience at Hades. I was alone and didn't have the posse' I have now. I didn't have the support that I have now. I wanted to fight him and I feel proud of what I did achieve but I couldn't do it alone. He was more powerful at influence than I was.

So how do you recognise an Alpha before you get bitten? This is the hardest one of all and I'm going to have to talk in general terms of some of the characteristics that I've found in my experience. Sadly, early on in your slaying career you may miss the signs and may get hurt. Hopefully the characteristics I mention below will assist you to find the hidden messages and the secret vampire beneath the charismatic exterior.

How to recognise an Alpha:

• Alphas are very charming with an ability to draw you in

• They tell you that they like and respect you, while you are achieving what they want

- They will give you feedback that you want to hear
- Generally they are intelligent or at least give the illusion of intelligence
- When people speak about them they say 'he knows his stuff, but I'm not sure I trust him'
- There is doubt about their abilities
- The longer you know them the more you can spot the negative aspects of personality
- They appear nice as pie one minute and then can explode at people the next minute
- They blame others for their mistakes
- They take leadership and power away from others
- They may use the 'I'm the boss that's why' kind of lines
- They 'pull rank' on you without notice
- They make self indulgent decisions
- They talk behind people's backs to gain your alliance

Sadly because alpha's are very good at 'playing human' you may not spot them until you are sucked in. Once sucked in you will experience the disappointment and hurt that comes with betrayal. The alpha doesn't believe that they are betraying you because they are so focused on positive outcomes for them selves that they fail to notice the collateral damage that occurs in their wake.

My biggest advice for dealing with alphas is don't fight for too long and don't take your inability to 'change them' as a personal failure. You won't change them and you won't save them. The only thing that can save an

Michelle T Holland

alpha is a tragic event in their own lives where they completely reassess who they are and their affect on others. By all means give it a go and try and help them to recover, but be willing to cut and run when they show their teeth.

Chapter 6: The Minion

I think the person who takes a job in order to live - that is to say, for the money - has turned himself into a slave. – Joseph Campbell

Many of the vampires that I had met in the past had a very aggressive nature. The Alpha who I have described already is an obvious and highly aggressive vampire. The thing is with vampires is that sometime they can be very passive as well. They can be harder to identify but they are vampire

Michelle T Holland

nonetheless. They still suck the life out of you if you engage too much with them.

Now saying that these vampires are not as destructive as the other vampires as far as people are concerned. They won't leave as many people in their wake. They will not create the same kind of personal or emotional damage. However damage is done by these to productivity and the ability to get things done.

Let me tell you about a particular vampire that I met a couple of years ago that I am going to call 'the Minion'.

In short, a minion is a people pleasure. I know it seems a little counterintuitive for a vampire to be a pleaser because you expect vampires to be mean. Here's one of the tricks in vampire slaying. Sometimes the nice ones are vampires too. Like I said they suck productivity out of a business, rather than the life out of someone, but it still…well…sucks.

This minion was a manager. She was around about 40 years of age. She had been in her position for a number of years. She knew her stuff and she knew it well. She always wanted to be the best at what she did. She also wanted everyone to know that she was good at what she did and that they recognised her for the work that she performed. These are all great qualities.

The main problem with the minion is they try to over pleased. They try so hard to please that they become a perfectionist. They are so concerned that they will not be seen as getting everything right that they begin to reduce the amount that they get done. They also end up stopping others from getting their work done. The minion's sense of approval is high. They must be liked; they must do the right thing by everyone.

Unearthing Vampires

Of course there was nothing wrong with this lady other than she was a vampire.

She was seen as a performer because she said the right things. She always said yes to the boss. Vampires like her can fly under the radar of your average person but not a skilled Slayer. I spotted her straight away.

I was asked by a Slayer in training to come into their company because she was aware of a number of vampires in their customer group and felt the business needed skills to deal with them. She also thought that there were a few vampires within the business that she hadn't found and needed a bit of assistance in identifying them. The Slayer in training was concerned because the productivity of the business wasn't as high as it should be so she knew that their must be vampires in the office. Here's a tip…if productivity and performance is low in your business then you have vampires.

I arrived on a Wednesday afternoon. It was a financial services company that I will call Minion Bank. The reception area of the business was no different than other financial services companies. They had marketing materials placed strategically. The posters on the walls showed happy smiling people enjoying a life of financial independence. On the wall behind the reception centre showed the exposed values of the business. I would quickly find out that like many businesses, the values written were not necessarily the values rewarded.

I told the receptionist who I was here to see and waited patiently for my colleague to come and take me into the business.

The Slayer in training came though a door and smiled with her hand extended. I shook her hand and followed her through the doors into the back offices of this company

The Slayer in training had told everyone that I was there to train the customer service officers, to be better customer service officers. They had their own vampires to slay so I was there to teach them how. Within the first hour of my time at Minion Bank I met the Minion. She was the manager of the customer service centre. When I met her she shook my hand, she said hello, and she was very pleasant. Minions may be people that other people would describe as nice. Nice is a funny word. I've always thought of it as an under done compliment. Its something you say about people when there's not much else to say about them.

The Minion was nice and people thought she was 'nice'.

I began speaking with the minion about her team, about what she wanted to achieve from this training program with her customer service officers. I knew what I wanted to achieve. I knew what the Slayer in training wanted to achieve. I knew what CEO of the organization wanted to achieve and I wanted to get her opinion. She was the manager after all, it was up to her to make sure that are customer officers follow through with all of the training after I left.

"So tell me what are you hoping to achieve from this customer service training?" Her response was not something that you would expect from a functional manager.

"Oh, I am not really sure. I really just want our customer service team to not get into trouble anymore. It will be great if we didn't get any complaints anymore. I really don't like having to talk to our senior managers about all the complaints that I am keep getting about my customer service team."

"Okay." I said. "Is handling difficult customers something that needs to be addressed."

"I guess so. Personally, I think they just need to be nicer." She replied.

"They need to be nicer to the customer?" I asked.

"Yes, the customers and each other and me, they just need to be nicer." She responded.

"So tell me what "nicer" would look like to you." I wanted to understand her definition of nice.

"Basically if they just did what the customer asked them to do and did what I asked them to do without trying to think too much about it. I think that would be better. The customer is always right as they say." She smiled at me looking for validation of what she had said.

"Its definitely important to provide what your customer needs and its important to provide them with leadership sometimes. What happens when a demanding customers comes into the centre and requests something that really can't happen." I asked.

"Well, they will generally tell the customer no and if the customer argues then they come and get me to handle it."

"And how do you handle it."

"I find out what the issue is and I tell the customer that the customer service staff is just following procedure but that I can do what they need done. I then go and fix whatever the issue is. I find its best to just do as the customer requests because it saves getting into an argument with them." She replied. I could see that she was pondering her answer. She just told me that she actively undermines her staff in front of the customer. No wonder there wasn't a lot of motivation or engagement in the customer centre.

"Do you think that resolving an issue always requires the other person getting what they want or is there an ability for you to influence them to compromise? What about if what they want is against company policy?" I was curious.

"Well, it pays to be nice and I don't want to upset them. If its totally against company policy then I defer the request to my boss so that they can tell the customer no. I don't like having to be the bad guy." I was starting to see the problem here. She was trying to turn the customer service team into vampires.

Now the thing is with being nice all the time and not standing up for yourself, your team and your business is that you become a Minion. Nice doesn't always get the right job done. A minion always appears busy. When you are trying to please people all the time you will appear very busy. Busy is not necessarily productive. It's very easy to become a minion vampire.

Now this person was not aggressive or destructive other than she was undermining her staff because she was trying to people please. She didn't realise that by trying to go out of her way to please the customer that she was not pleasing the staff member. This is the double standard and big problem with Minions. They work hard to please someone and end up upsetting someone else. This is very stressful for them.

The minion didn't speak at all about the key performance indicators of her team she just spoke about wanting to avoid conflict. I wanted to learn a bit more so I asked her about her role and what she did.

"So, tell me a little bit about you." I said. "What's your role?"

"Well I am the customer service manager." She looked at me with a confused look on her face.

"I am sorry I should have been a bit clear, I know what's your title is. I was just wondering what you did, how you contribute to the team success and what your customer service centre's staff would say about you. This is just useful to know before I go into a training session with a group of people. So, I am prepared, I like to be prepared for everything." I said to her.

"Well I, you know... I just, I listen to the staff and I just check up on them and make sure they are okay. I solve customer problems.... and well you know I just I...I..... Hmm......" I didn't even bother to ask her about the team's role. She struggled to answer what her value was never mind anybody else's. How is this woman is a manager of people? Through our whole conversation she didn't once mention about anything about performance or productivity.

This is the thing with minions. Minions tend to not have a specific plan in place and they may struggle to articulate their actual value and contribution to the business. The reason that they don't have a clear response is because they tend to wait to be told what to do. They are minion after all. They are not proactive and respond in the way that they think that the person wants them to respond. She struggled to answer me because she wasn't sure what I wanted to hear.

Michelle T Holland

This is why the minions are really hard to spot by your unassuming Slayer. Because you may think that they are doing a lot of work and they probably are. The problem is that the work they are doing is generally a lot of busy work and sometimes work that should be completed by someone else. Unfortunately because they are minions they will just do what they are told. They won't challenge the person who is allocating the work. They won't challenge the team to do more. When you are a minion your productivity is low. Busyness is high but productivity is low.

The good thing about the minion is that they can be saved.

After my meeting with the Minion I went and spoke to the Slayer in training.

"Your problem is not that the customer service centre staff don't know how to deal with vampires. The problem is that your customer services manager is a vampire called a Minion."

"But she's so nice." She look shocked and I smiled. "Ok, your smile tells me that this is a characteristic of a Minion vampire. How can I identify them in the future?"

Ways to spot a Minion:
- They are described regularly as nice.
- They always appear really busy but never seem to achieve their performance plan.
- They are known as the person who will say yes to anything.
- They have a tendency to undermine their team by 'solving a problem' that may not exist.

46

- They avoid conflict as much as possible.
- They will side with a bully or vampire over a human because they don't want to get into conflict with the vampire.
- They don't address poor behaviours in a constructive way.
- They are busy…not productive.

"Oh boy, that's definitely the manager. How did I not see this before? We always just looked at the team and figured that they were lacking in skills. But I can see now that she has contributed to this by not allowing the staff member to control the situation. She always sends the problems up the line and expects her staff to do the same thing. She is not achieving the outcomes for the business that are needed because she's so busy pleasing customers that really should be managed and sent on their way." I smiled at her revelation. She was right. At times you need to 'fire' your clients if they are not contributing to the success of the business. The minion was keeping the vampire customers happy instead of working on the skills of her team to manage the poor vampire behaviours. "Right, so how do we fix this?"

"You need to change which behaviours are being rewarded. The expectations that you have of her need to change and she needs to be supported while she changes her behaviour and learns new skills. This won't happen quickly but its possible. It all depends if you want to invest in changing her."

"Yes, we want to invest in her. I'd like to work with her to see if I can save this vampire. I think it would be a good outcome for her team, the business and me if I can help her to change her behaviours."

"I agree."

This situation was able to be saved through improving the manager's behaviour, the skills of the team, the expectations of the business and the processes that the customer service team used.

A final word on this vampire. Many times Minion Vampires can be saved and many times they cannot and therefore need to be removed from the business. They are definitely a vampire that you want to invest the time and effort in trying to reform.

Chapter 7: The High Maintenance Life Sucking Vampire

I want a cheeseburger so badly, but I have to be a vampire in a few weeks.
– Kristen Stewart

All vampires drain your energy. This is one of the tell tale signs that you are dealing with a vampire of course however I encountered a particularly draining vampire a few years ago that I think is worth a separate discussion.

She was a young up and coming professional in a business that I worked in for a while. On face value she appeared to be a lovely person and I became very friendly with this person until I recognised the vampire that she was. Let me tell you the story.

It was an office environment and this 'girl' was working as a training officer. She had come highly recommended and had impressive degrees so when I met her I was, like others, impressed by her. I was working on a training contract for a short period of time doing some work with her and a few others in her team.

After a week or two we had become quite friendly. Regularly chatting about this or that. I was impressed with her capabilities and the way she spoke turned my 'potential Slayer' radar on.

One day after a particularly long week she started to tell me about one of the other members of the team who she didn't get along with. This is not unusual in an office environment so I didn't really pay much attention to it. She spoke about this one member 'taking credit' for a job she had done and was quiet upset by the interaction. I was also working with this person and was surprised at the story she told. She was very upset by it so I comforted her and gave her some advice for dealing with it, including going to the person and speaking with them about it.

About a week later, she came to me again talking to me about an interaction that she'd had with a general manager in the business and how this general manager didn't respond to her suggestions the way that she thought they should. Again she became quite upset by the interaction and was visible shaken by the event. Again I gave her advice and told her to speak with the person. I even offered my support if she needed it. I was pretty sure the general manager wasn't a vampire but you can never be too careful.

The occurrences of her seeking my 'advice' became more and more frequent until I became exhausted just at the thought of interacting with her. She told me about her background which included many 'tragic' incidents. She spoke to me about her frustrations in her personal relationship. She told me about every interaction in the workplace that left her 'frustrated and disappointed'. After a number of months working with this person I realised that she was a vampire and one of the worst kinds. She was a 'HMLS' (high maintenance life sucker). You will experience these vampires regularly in the workplace and if you don't slay them quickly they will slowly drain the life out of you.

She wanted to run her own show, she wanted to do the training her way, and decided that the way I was running things was not for her. Instead of talking to me, she did the vampire thing and avoided the work, undermined me and her team, and created an unhealthy work environment by complaining about and to higher level managers and her peers. Her immaturity was regularly on display. She cried and complained to many of the young men in the building who supported her because they were dazzled by her blond hair and vulnerability.

I hadn't realised how much energy and life she was draining from me until I finally recognised her as a vampire and stopped my interaction. I also didn't realise the affect she was having on others in the business until after she was slain. A number of the people that she was complaining about to me (ie: the other member of the team and the general manager) were also experiencing the same life draining activities. They told me that she was complaining about me not helping her enough!

These vampires are actually easy to spot as long as you see the symptoms early enough. If you leave it late then they start to suck the life out of you and let me tell you, its hard to see vampire behaviours when you are exhausted.

The way to spot a 'HMLS' early on is to recognise the following behaviours:

- They complain about many others and disguise it as 'trying to understand', including loved ones
- They regularly have a 'sad' story to tell
- They tell stories of many past injustices, to anyone who will listen
- They are usually highly educated
- They may come from a home life where there was too much or too little attention
- They may appear to be an over achiever, but fail to achieve practical outcomes
- They talk a lot about what they can do and what they want to do but again, have limited outcomes
- They play people off against each other

- Other people tell you that they are 'draining' to work with
- You are always giving them advice, that they rarely take
- You feel tired after speaking with them
- They gather support from other areas that don't work with them directly

Interactions with others should leave you feeling energised and thankful for the interaction. If there is a person that you have in your life that is draining your energy and you continue to interact with them because of your relationship or because you feel sorry for them. You may be dealing with a 'HMLS' vampire. You may be able to save this vampire if they are only infected on a minor level. If they don't recognise a need to change then slay and get out before they suck the life completely out of you.

Michelle T Holland

Chapter 8: The Immortals

It is not strange... to mistake change for progress. – Millard Fillmore

Immortals are everywhere. They are dangerous and you can spot them from a mile away. They are also hard to deal with because they are very skilled in avoiding both being saved and slain. Also they are very skilled in finding ways of becoming protected.

Often Immortals feel discomfort in private enterprises because of the pace at which private business moves so you are less likely to experience one there. If you do come across an Immortal in private business its generally because of a family connection to the boss.

Let me tell you where you generally find Immortals. In government style organisations. These might be government departments or organisations that are affiliated strongly with the government. Immortals are found in large numbers and in concentrated pockets of these organisations.

The reason that they are generally found in these kinds of organisations is because of a few reasons. These organisations are often run by Immortals and there are usually less Slayers. In organisations where there are a large concentration of Immortals it becomes very uncomfortable to be a Slayer because their competencies are not generally the ones rewarded.

An Immortal is a vampire who has out lasted most other people and Slayers in the organisation. They are generally of an older generation and they have been in the same organisation for at least 15 years or more. A big word of warning when identifying these vampires. Not everyone who has been in an organisation for over 15 years and not everyone who works in a government organisation is an Immortal. Immortals have a very clear set of characteristics that set them apart from others who may actually enjoy the organisation and their work, hence the longevity.

An Immortal that I met about 6 years ago will show you the difference between a long serving human and an Immortal vampire.

This Immortal's name was Greg. Greg had been working in the same organisation for 10 years. Now on the surface you would say that he doesn't meet the criteria but when you dig a bit deeper into Greg's history you find that he has been working in the same industry and the same kind of job for over 20 years. Although he'd moved organisations he had moved to be with the same boss that he'd had at the previous organisation.

Greg was a frustration to many other people that he worked with. Greg was in a senior management role so his influence and authority was formal, and yet his ability to influence was minimal. This is because there were a number of Slayers in this organisation which made it difficult for Greg to remain hidden. The funny thing about Immortals is just when you think they have been uncovered they do something to hide again.

Greg was very good at convincing the management of the organisation that he was good at his job. He was clever at stacking his team with high performing employees and he was clever about taking the credit for their good work. The management didn't seem to mind that the high performing employees would not stay very long and Greg was often recruiting for more.

This is the way that Greg stayed under the radar. He was good at recruiting people who worked hard and could make him look good. When they left Greg didn't look at himself and his behaviour instead his reason was generally the same. "I recruit them just out of University and once they have some experience they move on to higher paid

Michelle T Holland

jobs." He even had me convinced early on and I've met many Immortals.

Greg was a lovely person, when he wasn't sucking the productivity out of the business. He was likeable so he got away with under performing. He flew under the radar and he had invested in good relationships in the business to ensure that he went relatively unnoticed.

I remember having a conversation with the CEO of the company and spoke to him about Greg. The respond from the CEO was typical when talking about Immortals; he sad to me. "Yes, I know that Greg doesn't perform as well as other managers in the business but he's harmless and he has been here forever….what are you going to do?" shrug…

Well dude, what you do is you save them or slay them. Immortals are not 'harmless'. They suck the productivity out of a business and they cause other high performing managers to question 'why they bother?' They affect the culture in a major way and need to be dealt with.

To tell the difference between a long serving employee and an Immortal look for someone:

- that others complain about regularly;
- that seems to get away with not doing a lot;
- who is friendly and talks a lot;
- who has a way of getting 'out of trouble'
- who flies under the radar
- who survives change after change
- that is seen at every organisational event
- that seems to be positive about every thing the CEO releases

• that rarely make changes to their work and never challenge senior management

• They usually have a team of frustrated employees or colleagues doing all the work

These vampires are hard to save because they have survived for so long by being an Immortal. You may need to make a call on the severity of their vampirism. If its mild and they are truly 'harmless' move on to more draining and threatening vampires....believe me the Immortal will be there when you've finished with the others.

Michelle T Holland

Chapter 9: The Golden Child

People are motivated by the desires for privilege, for power, for profit. Those are not shocking revelations. Anyone who's had any experience in life knows these things. – Norman Finkelstein

You've met the golden child. I told you the story about my time at 'Hades' so you've met the one I knew well. There is a golden child in almost every company so I suspect you know one yourself.

The golden child is that person that you see in the business who appears to be doing nothing, and yet still manages to progress through the ranks of the business.

They seem to enthral the business leaders with their charm and can get away with murder.

They appear to be doing nothing particularly wrong, and nothing particularly good. They have the ear of the boss. They appear to have the confidence of the business leaders and you are not really sure why. They do just enough to get by and they are really well liked by the senior management. As a hard worker who achieves great things for the business you find it hard to understand why these people are so well liked.

The difficultly you will face identifying this vampire is that it's important to be well liked in a business. We all want to be liked and have great relationships. Great relationships help the work flow through the business. In fact, relationships are a key element of the Slayer codex. The difference between a human and a Slayer creating great relationships and the golden child, is motivation and outcomes.

The Slayer and the human focuses on creating real sustainable relationships that help them to achieve outcomes for the business and the businesses customers. They work to build relationships to enable collaboration and successful work outcomes for the team. They are liked and likeable, and they get great things done.

The golden child is more focused on the relationship than getting the job done. They don't tend to work towards meaningful outcomes because they are not willing to challenge the bosses. They are willing to produce a lower quality outcome rather than risk the boss being unhappy with them. They know that by challenging the boss will damage the relationship, and this is the higher risk for them.

At times we all 'chose our battles' and decide that challenging something is worth the fight, or the damage it may do to the relationship. This is different motivation again. We tend to do this to save the relationship for the relationships sake, because it is important to us. We respect and like the other person and determine that the challenge won't result in a big enough gain to risk the relationship. The motivation for the golden child is to save the relationship because the relationship keeps them safe. They know that if that relationship is damaged then their quality of life at work will be very different. They also don't tend to make this same decision for all relationships. The golden child will happily drop a colleague in the poo and spoil that relationship if it means keeping their relationship with the boss in tact. The Gold Child is focused on relationships that provide him something person, eg power, money, status, or safety.

The GC at 'Hades' wouldn't challenge Vincent. It didn't matter whether he believed in it or not, he would say yes to Vincent. He would agree and Vincent liked him of course, because he was an Alpha and did not like people disagreeing or challenging him. You will find lot of GCs, and wannabe GCs, in organisation that have an Alpha sitting in the top position. Hostile dominance attracts passive agreers, and vice versa.

Let me tell you a story of another golden child. He was an executive assistant to the CEO of a very large business. He worked for them for a number of years and on the surface it appeared that he did what he needed to do. He was very well liked by the CEO because he worked hard to stay out of trouble. He would give her the information that she needed and he would give her information that was tantalizing as well. This CEO liked a little bit of gossip. She was a great leader, but like all of us she had her Achilles Heel. She liked to know what is going on in the organization and the juicier the better. So he kept her high on gossip. He became her dealer and she loved him for it.

I want to make a point here, just so that you remember not to demonize this woman. We all have a vampire in us and our vamp will find the area of our lives that is the most vulnerable. For this woman it was an insecurity of not knowing all of the information and being unable to answer a question by someone on the board, or one of her direct reports, or the media. This led her to being overly concerned in what was happening in the organisation and needing a lot of information. The vampire inside of her that liked to distract her from her mission with gossip and was being assisted by an external vampire that used this vulnerability for his own purposes.

Sadly, this is how many humans can be led over to the dark side (thank you George Lucas). When our vampire inside is being supported by a vampire on the outside it is a recipe for disaster for the human. You see this play out in so many people's lives. From the woman who wants to lose weight only to have her husband continually order take away and take her out for meals, to the drug addicted teenager who is handed money by a well-meaning, yet uneducated parent. The vampires of our world conspire to stop us from living and achieving our mission. They are cunning creatures that will stop at nothing to distract you from your calling.

Back to our GC of the moment. Other people in the business didn't understand what his role was, they couldn't see the value that he was adding to the business and they thought he was highly paid for the kind of work that he was actually doing. What they didn't see was fact that he had worked out the boss's particular vintage of vampirism. She wanted to know information and he gave that to her. This the skill of the golden child, they figure out very quickly what makes the boss tick and how to use it for their personal gain.

Although his competency wasn't high, he flew under the raider and got just enough done not to look incompetent, while feeding her vampire. Therefore, when he asked for a pay rise he got it, when he asked his boss for a new promotion into a different position because he had an interest in doing it she gave it to him. This person is now in a very senior position in this organization. The CEO has since moved on and he has become the golden child for another senior manager who is obviously battling their own vampire. What he lacked in business competency he made up in GC skill.

Allowing yourself to be vulnerable is an important part of being human and an important part of being a good Slayer. However, where a Slayer uses vulnerability to stop hiding from pain, and to connect with others, the vampire uses it as a way of tempting the human into becoming a vampire.

The GC is a yes person, they will do what ever sucking up is needed to become successful. Being a nice, helpful person is a great quality to have, it's when it crosses over into becoming a door mat, or a yes person that it is damaging. When you are constantly saying yes to someone else, then you are saying no to you and the meaningful work that you were put on the earth to achieve. If you meet someone, or are someone, who consistently puts others ahead of themselves and is not achieving anything for themselves or their business then you are probably dealing with a minion. When you see someone that appears to do this only for the higher level managers, and seems to be achieving great successes for themselves, but not others, then that would be a GC.

Here are a few ways you can recognize a golden child quickly:

1. They fly under the raider and get enough done to meet performance expectations,
2. They are really well liked by the senior management,
3. They don't appear to get a lot of meaningful outcomes yet they are always selected to be on organizational committees and project teams,
4. They have the ear of the CEO/Senior Manager,
5. The CEO or the senior manager talks about their personal characteristics in a

very positive way, and fails to mention their outcomes.

6. Other people wonder how they have become so successful.
7. They focus their energy on getting to know a new senior manager well.
8. They don't treat staff lower on the organizational chart very well, unless they too have a very good relationship with the CEO or bosses.

These kind of vampires they drain the work out of the business. When they are very skilled as a GC they can help a culture of 'them and us' to thrive. You need to be aware of them. You need to be able to find them as soon as you can because the other thing the golden child can be is a great ally for potential Slayer. If you can get them on board, if you can get them over to your side, they can use their influence for good rather than evil.

Michelle T Holland

Chapter 10: The Younglings

A person's a person, no matter how small. – Dr. Seuss

I know that when you hear this name you think "I'm a Slayer, this will be easy. They are young, they are inexperience, they are immature. What harm could they be doing?" Well again like other vampires they have a special way of being able to drain the life out of you. They can also suck the business out of the business.

The warning for you when you come up against a Youngling is they will draw your energy away and they

Michelle T Holland

will take your focus, and you will want to give it to them. The mere fact that they are young means you will be drawn to help them. They are vulnerable to evil, but unlike many vampires if you get to them early enough you can help them change and they have the potential to become great Slayers.

In my experience with the Younglings, is that I've saved many more than I've slain. This is because they become vampires through inexperience, immaturity and ignorance. Many Younglings start their journey into the vampire world because of experiences that they have had with parents, peers, university lecturers or early bosses. They may not have the strength that they need to escape the vampire pull. They may be distracted easily from purpose because they are yet to firmly establish and believe in their purpose. Low self-esteem, particularly in young women, is a ripe doorway for a vampire to walk through. This is why it's so important as parents to protect your children from the vampire by building their sense of independence, confidence and esteem.

When you find a Youngling in an organization it's easy to ignore them and think they aren't causing any problems. Unfortunately, in a business where Younglings go unchecked, they may become another kind of vampire, such as a Minion or a HMLS. When you find a Youngling I urge you to put time and energy into discovering if they can be saved.

Let me tell you a story about a Youngling that a friend of mine worked with. This friend of mine is a Slayer, a very experienced Slayer and had worked with Younglings before. It took her a while to recognize this particular Youngling because the Youngling wasn't in the same category of Younglings as she met before. The Youngling had come to the Slayer's team with great references and a wonderful recruitment process. They appeared to have a good head on their shoulders and didn't come across as a traditional Youngling.

It's easy to miss the signs of the Youngling, particularly if they have been raised by other vampires. They are clever and deceptive. Sadly, the Younglings don't realise that they are being deceptive because the behaviour that they display is the behaviour that has been rewarded by vampires in their life. Its only when they enter the world of the Slayer that they start to struggle. Through this struggle you will recognize them as a Youngling about a transition into becoming a more dangerous vampire.

Let me give you the highlights of the story. We'll call the Youngling Jennifer. Jennifer was quite an experienced professional, she has been working in that area of accounting for a couple of years. She had great qualifications, she knew what she was doing, and she had worked for quite big organization before my friend hired her. She came with glowing references. She appeared to be the perfect person.

Its common in recruitment processes to confuse and baffle ourselves. We get a false sense of security and misunderstand what we are actually trying to achieve. This usually happens when we see someone that we think is similar to us. Seeing our reflection in others is a sign of our own vampire trying to distract us.

On reflection my friend noted a feeling that the Youngling may be too good to be true, and that she may be too reliant on others. Her initial Slayer sense suspected that this person may be a Minion, but it wasn't strong enough to worry about. Unfortunately, even the savviest of managers can get tricked to hiring someone because they remind them of themselves. She liked Jennifer, and just put the dependence feeling down to her age. She saw herself in Jennifer and thought she could mentor her. So she decided to take a chance and she hired this person.

Generally, this is the right thing to do with a Youngling. Take a chance on them. After six months, the problems started to appear. She noticed small things at first, a complaint here or there from another team mate about Jennifer. She then noticed Jennifer 'forgetting' to organize specific parts of her work. After a few months of small performance concerns my friend addressed it with Jennifer, only to have her burst in to tears. My friend liked Jennifer so continued to give her the benefit of the doubt.

After an incident that resulted in the board financial papers almost not getting to the board, my Slayer friend was at her wits end. She decided to look through the recruitment process and paperwork to see how she had made such a mistake with this person. When my friend reviewed the psychometric assessment that she had engaged but failed to review on hiring she saw plainly the mistake she'd made. The assessment showed a confused individual who was highly dependent, ambitious and did not accept developmental feedback.

She made a mistake by ignoring the behaviour of this Youngling for too long. The Slayer unfortunately ended up in having to leave the organization because the Youngling teamed up with an Immortal who made her life terrible.

The Immortal took advantage of the Youngling's inexperience and vulnerability. Through information that the Youngling provided to him, he made sure it was too uncomfortable for the Slayer to stay. She came to me a very broken Slayer. Upset and hurt that she wasn't able to see the challenges placed in front of her with the Youngling. She knew the Immortal was out to get her, but she had trusted the Youngling.

The best of us can get side swiped by vampires. She allowed herself to be dragged down by the negative vibes around her. She wasn't able to lift herself above the situation to view what was happening and what she was doing to contribute to the situation. This is a really tough thing to do as I've mentioned before, it's not easy being a Slayer. It's bloody rewarding but it's not easy.

When I asked her on reflection what she could have done differently, she saw completely, clearly, and straightaway that she needed to bring the Youngling under her wing and create her into a new Slayer. She failed to do that. She could give many reasons that she didn't, her busy schedule, her own insecurities, her misguided trust, but ultimately she made a mistake and opened the door for the Immortal vampire to get in and convert this Youngling. The Youngling was searching for a mentor. She was seeking someone to help her grow. Sadly, the vampire got to her and offered her what she was seeking before the Slayer did.

Younglings can be destructive in an organization because of their immaturity. They don't realize that damage they are doing until too late. The more immaturity that they have, the more mistakes that they make and the closer they become into becoming the vampire. It's really important as Slayers to be able to see these Younglings, it's really important to catch the behaviour before it blossoms into a vampire.

Throughout my journey as a Slayer, I've made it my mission to get to these Younglings before they become vampires. There are so many Alphas and Immortals just waiting to infect the Youngling with their toxins. Your role as a Slayer is to help create Slayers for the future. The Youngling and Potential Slayers are where you should focus the most of your energy. They are the Slayers of the future and the more we are able to catch these Younglings before the other vampires infect them the better. If we want a different future, where the Slayer is much more common than the vampire in businesses, in life, in politics then we need to make sure that every Youngling that we can save from becoming a vampire is saved. Every person that has the aptitude to be a potential Slayer is given the opportunity to release their Slayer.

If you have a Youngling in your team right now then at least buy them this book as a gift and send them on start of their journey on becoming a Slayer. Take them under your wing, make sure they have the understanding and the development to maturity to be able to be a great Slayer.

A word of warning. Some Younglings have been raised by vampires who are truly terrible. They many have an Alpha as a mother or a father, or worse, a truly evil one (TEO) – I'll talk about them soon. Where this is the case, unless you are a qualified psychologist I would slay quickly. Remove them from your life and send them towards someone that can help them. A Youngling raised by a TEO is one of life's tragedies and requires specialized intervention.

Unearthing Vampires

The Younglings, humans and potential Slayers are our future. My challenge to you is here, as soon as you unleash your own inner Slayer, as soon as you step forward and become a Slayer, I want you to pay it forward to other people in your work place and life. For every Youngling that you save there is one less potential Alpha, Golden Child or Immortal terrorizing your organization.

Michelle T Holland

Michelle T Holland

Chapter 11: The Truly Evil One

Most of the evil in this world is done by people with good intentions.—T.S. Eliot

I've left this one to last because they are the most destructive and they are the hardest to slay. I'm very sad to report that there are some vampires in the world that are unsaveable. These vampires display such atrocious behaviours and attributes that my only advice is try everything you can and then slay, ie: cut and run.

Eventually their toxins will become so intense within their bodies that they will self-destruct. They will either make themselves sick from all the toxins or they will eventually burn their business to the ground, metaphorically speaking of course.

Michelle T Holland

However, until this happens the best thing for any self-respecting Slayer to do is leave. These vampires are different than the Alpha. Alphas are pretty bad, but there is still a shred of human in them and with serious work they can be managed. Not saved necessarily, but managed.

The Truly Evil Ones cannot be saved. They are too far gone for us and if they are to be saved they would require significant intervention from someone skilled in managing evil behaviours. I'm not sure even Van Helsing could manage some of them. Let me tell you a story about a human friend of mine and his Evil Vampire boss.

My friend Jack worked for a man that we'll just call Teo (truly evil one). Teo owned a business that specialised in heavy earth movers. You know those really massive trucks and machines that they use in the mines? Jack was the crew boss and had a very important job in coordinating not just the crew, but also the clients.

Teo hired Jack because he knew that Jack was really good with managing big contracts and could get them completed efficiently and at a great profit margin. Before Jack started, Teo's business was about to go into insolvency and Teo was at a point whereby the contracts that he had won last year he was set to loose, because people didn't like to work with him. Teo knew that to have a successful business and continue to pay for his shiny Porsche he needed someone to take care of the problems. So he found and hired Jack.

Jack worked really hard for Teo and managed to win back a number of the big clients that Teo had already alienated. Jack was a very successful employee and worked hard for Teo.

After working hard for 12 months, Jack started to notice something changing in Teo. Teo was making really good money from the business with Jack in charge. Jack asked Teo to invest in the business now that they were in the black again. They required new tools and equipment to manage the contracts and maintenance that they had. Some of the items of equipment were becoming unsafe to use and Jack was concerned that they would injure someone. Teo wasn't interested in spending money on tools. He preferred to spend his money on fancy cars and fancy women.

After summing up his courage Jack decided to confront Teo and spoke to him about the tools and equipment that was required, he told Teo about compliance issues that needed addressing, and he spoke about the crew needing some more support because they were loosing motivation. Teo wasn't interested in listening to Jack. He told Jack to just ignore the broken machinery and asked Jack to do a number of things that Jack felt were immoral at the least, illegal at the worst. Jack refused and Teo continued to put pressure on him.

Teo moved Jack to another worksite that was even more dangerous than the other. Jack spoke to Teo and Teo proceeded to ignore all of his communication.

On a bright sunny day, Jack went into work and while there fell off of one of the trucks because of a broken part that Jack had told Teo about. Jack lay in the dirt for a while with a broken shoulder wondering how his life had taken such a rough turn. He'd worked damn hard for this man to create a business that was now turning over a healthy profit where a year ago was heading to closure. Now, Jack was lying in the dirt, broken and hurt -

physically and emotionally. He'd done everything right and ended up broken.

Eventually one of the crew found Jack and took him to the hospital in Jack's company car.

While in hospital, Jack developed a collapsed lung and couldn't get back to work. He spoke to Teo and told him that he'd be off work for a period of 3 weeks while he recovered.

Teo, being the evil vampire he was, told Jack that he wanted the company car back and also refused to pay him his sick pay or time in lieu that he'd promised. While Jack was still in hospital recovering from the shoulder and collapsed lung Teo picked up the car and sold it.

Jack knew this wasn't right as the car was part of his contract of employment so he asked for it back. Teo obviously didn't like this so he sent a letter back to Jack telling him that his services were no longer required. Jack, a loyal and hard working employee, who had done nothing but create a profitable business for Teo was now in hospital, broken, unwell and out of work.

There is no reasoning with evil creatures like Teo. They think that because they own a business and have given people jobs that they can treat people the way they choose. Which is often terrible and cruel.

One of the scariest things with the TEOs of the world is that they are really hard to spot upfront. This is because part of their truly evilness is in drawing you in to their lives and making you believe that they need and respect you before ripping everything away. They are generally underhanded but their actions once they reveal themselves is consistent.

Unearthing Vampires

Here are a few ways to spot a TEO:

- they rely on others to create success for them;

- people tell you that they are evil;

- something doesn't feel right when you are working with them;

- they may have done some truly despicable things in the past;

- they are willing and able to sack someone without cause;

- they don't support their people if something major happens in their lives;

- they rarely, if ever, give positive feedback to their crew; and

- the tell you hardship secrets about other people/businesses with an evil delight.

As I said, do your best to use the Slay or Save methods to manage these vampires and then don't feel bad when they don't change and you need to let it go.

Sad and disappointing as it is the best thing to do with Teo is to leave or have them leave. If they report to you remove them quickly. If you report to them…run!

Michelle T Holland

Chapter 12: Three Big Vampire Tricks

Of course it is happening inside your head, Harry, but why on earth should that mean that it is not real? Said Dumbledore — J.K. Rowling (Harry Potter and the Deathly Hallows)

I want to briefly cover off three of the big tricks the vampires commonly deploy. These tricks can get the best of you if you are unaware of them. When you recognizing a vampire, you need to recognize its tricks as well. The last few chapters I've discussed the common vampires that you will regularly find in life and business, there are more of course, but these are the main ones that you'll find.

The tricks that they use are many and varied, however there are three tricks that they use regularly to get through life without being slayed, or saved. Keep your eyes open for these behaviours and you'll be able to slay or save the vampire, while keeping yourself safe from harm.

The Glamour

The glamour is a clever trick that vampires pull to keep them safe within an organisation. This one primarily is used by the Alpha, The GC, and the HMLS, but can be used by any vampire. Essentially, they convince people in the organisation that they are invaluable and likeable. They may even appear competent at what they are employed to do. Yet when you dig deeper you can see that they are not likeable, and they are not competent. You can generally see the glamour happening when you look hard enough.

When you observe someone in the work place who is not obviously likeable, and doesn't appear competent and yet they seem to be promoted regularly, and/or revered by management then you may be experiencing a glamour. As I described before, the GC is extraordinarily good at this trick. When the promotion or reverence is real and deserved you feel it in your bones, you don't question it. But when you start wondering what the heck is going on…that's when you need to dig deeper.

Some work places call this the political game. I call it a glamour. The vampires have figured out the game that is being played out in the organisation. Every organisation has a game, and every organisation has vampires playing it. In many organisations the slayers and the humans try to play the game, but they are never as successful as the vampires. So my advice is to just get on with the job of being authentic and you'll be able to notice when others are not.

Let's say at your organisation the game is about not getting into trouble. You'll know that this is the culture of the business because innovation is limited and people feel constrained by rules and process. Vampires love this kind of culture because they can survive easily by not creating change, not challenging the bosses, and just doing enough to met their performance expectations.

They will go out of their way to be seen as an essential part of the business. They generally do this is two ways. They will make sure that the right people like them, they won't take time to bother with other people, they don't care if you like them or not but they very much care if the CEO or the senior executive like them or not. They will find out how to create personal relationships with the people in charge and spend a lot of time maintaining these relationships. You'll see this happening when you talk to someone who is always too busy to help you or meet your expectations because they are 'doing something for the boss'.

Michelle T Holland

They are not concerned about being liked because of the outcomes what they achieve, meaningful work they could do, or the change they could make. They are very concerned with fitting in the organisation and staying safe. Vampires are primarily focused on staying safe, they tend not to challenge the status quo. They generally will only challenge the status quo if they are in a senior management position and they have the authority and power to do so. When they are not in a senior leadership position the only way that they feel they can influence is by using the glamour. So they go out of their way to make sure that the right people like them. They do just enough to get a great pay check and pats on the back by the boss, and nothing more. They don't take risk because they don't want things to get wrong and put their glamour at risk.

Lack of Reflection

You will know from the movies that Vampires have a lack of reflection. The movie shows a beautiful man standing in front of a shop window next to an unsuspecting victim. The victim smiles brilliantly at the vampire until they look sideways and see that they are not appearing in the window. They look back to the vampire and see the evil in their eyes and the sharpened teeth just before…you know how this story ends.

This is a literal interpretation of a lack of reflection. Unfortunately, it's not always that obvious in the workplace. It would be great if during recruitment or performance management you could just hold up a mirror and go 'Ah hah! Gotcha'.

You will see this trick playing out the workplace in various ways. A common method of discovery is when you observe someone who appears completely unaware of the impact that their behaviour has on the world.

They don't look in the mirror and see themselves within the problem, they only see the problem. This is obviously a big concern because if you can't reflect, you can't grow. So if you come across a vampire with no reflection, they are very hard vampires to save.

Another way of looking at this is called 'Locus of Control'. This was a concept introduced by psychologist Julian Rotter. This concept has been around for over 60 years and describes how someone 'copes' with the world around them. The theory essentially describes two types of people. Those that have an internal locus of control, which means that they believe that they are in control of their destiny or outcomes. For example if they succeed at something they will hold a sense of purpose and regard their achievement as being something that they influenced. If they fail then they believe that they had a contribution to the failure and seek to learn from this failure. Slayers, and many humans, will have an internal locus of control.

The other kind are those that have an external locus of control, which means that they believe that others are responsible for what happens to them. If they have a success they will take it for granted or say that they were lucky, and when they have a failure they will have a tendency to blame others or circumstances. They don't take responsibility for their own part in the failure and will look for the external influence. For example, if they are late to an event they will tell you about the traffic that they had to fight, and they may comment about absurdity of the start time of the event, without even acknowledging that they took too long getting ready or that they took the wrong street. This is to distract people from blaming them. Vampires, and some immature humans, have an external locus of control.

There is an immaturity in having a lack of reflection. We come to expect children to blame their sister for making them angry because they are still learning about life. When an adult states that 'someone made my angry' or allow themselves to throw a tantrum in the office, it shows a lack of emotional intelligence and maturity.

Without this intelligence or maturity it can be hard for change to occur and they will continue to harm others.

I came across a particularly strong vampire a number of years ago. He was very strong and particularly difficult to deal with because he was a GC, with a strong desire to be the next Alpha. He had no reflection on his behaviour. Even when he was accused of bullying and harassment by a number of people in his team he could not reflect and see his contribution. I was asked to look at the circumstances behind the bullying and harassment it turned out that he had been behaving the same way a number of years. I discovered many people who had left the organisation because of his behaviour, and had never told anyone. When I spoke to them they said that they didn't feel safe telling anyone because he was the GC and protected.

The people who had instigated the bullying claim recognised the vampire behaviour and didn't want anyone else to experience it. When confronted with these behaviours he denied them. Even when a senior manager declared that they had witnessed an incident personally he excused the behaviour and said it was the result of torment from the others. He completely denied every accusation and turned the tables on the instigators saying that they were lying to get him in trouble and he was the victim. He put in a formal complaint about them bullying him as a deflection. At no point did he ever say that he had any role to play. All of the other's questions spoke of their part in the relationship and expressed remorse over their behaviour. The vampire, however, never looked at his own reflection.

Michelle T Holland

Generally the remedy for this trick is to help the vampire to see their behaviour reflected by others and help them to understand the impact that its having on them. A behaviour assessment tool and a 360 degree feedback process is often enough for a vampire to see the impact they are having and begin the process of being saved.

If they never see their reflection, or understand the impact that they are having on others then they will never grow and develop and they will never be saved.

The Compelling Charm

The third trick is a very interesting trick and it works well with the glamour. This trick you see a lot in vampires like the GC, they tend to compel other people to do their jobs for them and they can do this through charm.

However, the Alpha is the expert in this trick. They are generally surrounded by Minions, Younglings and other followers like the GC. A strong Alpha is no match for the weaker vampires. Other than the Immortal of course. The Immortal is often immune to this kind of behaviour because they have been around for so long that

they don't need to be compelled to do the Alpha's bidding. The Immortal will follow the Alpha merely because they are the Alpha.

We often see the ability to take charge, or take the lead as being a positive thing in our leaders. We want them to set a clear vision and help us to achieve great things by leading the way. When we observe a great leader taking charge we want to follow them because they inspire us with their behaviour and vision. When the Alpha takes charge, they take from other people. They don't inspire, rather they command. When someone says to you "take the lead", leadership is being offered to you. Generally you are offered leadership when you have displayed qualities to that person or persons that show you will keep them safe and you will show them a better way.

Taking the lead without the offer can sometimes be seen as a dominant display by an Alpha. If you take the lead, you must be aware that you could be taking it from somebody else. This is how Alpha vampires behave. They walk into an organisation and they *take* the lead, and often take it away from other. They want control and therefore they take control in an authoritarian way. They hold the power position within the organisation and therefore they believe that everyone should do as they say. When someone stands up to them they shut them down quickly because they believe that leadership is about command and control.

An Alpha vampire can be very charming, so they are able to compel people to do work for them. At times they compel them through strength, at times they compel them through charm. The problem with the Alpha that compels through charm is that when they don't get their own way, they retaliate and take control through the power of their position. When you are being charmed by an Alpha it is important that you know that you are only one step from being step on.

Alpha's charm and control, what they don't do is collaborate. The Alpha does not like leaders who argue with them. This is because they need to be in control to feel valuable. There are many reasons for this behaviour which I won't go into now. Regardless of the reason, what you need to know is that people act like this in business and in life and you have to be prepared for it. If you get the opportunity to work on saving an Alpha you can find out everything you need to know about the root cause of their behaviour.

Influence is a good thing, compelling is not influencing. The ideal situation is that people are influenced for the greater good. Vampires are selfish, so generally they compel for their own outcomes, such as personal status and achievements that they can take credit for.

Slayers and humans use influencing skills to encourage a new kind of culture and relationships. The difference between them and vampires is that they work for the greater good.

Part 3: How to 'Slay' or 'Save' the Vampires

"The only thing necessary for the triumph of evil is for good men to do nothing."
— Edmund Burke

CUSTOMERS ARE FOR SELLING NOT SUCKING

Michelle T Holland

To save or to slay that is the question.

Let's first talk about what I mean by saving and slaying before we answer that question.

Saving should always be your first protocol. My philosophy is that every person deserves a chance. Even if they displaying vampire tendencies. I say this seriously because I know that humans, and slayers, develop vampire tendencies and display vampire behaviours for a reason. The reason may not be completely evident to you in the moment that you are confronted by them, but there is always a reason.

Perhaps they had an abusive upbringing, perhaps they lost a puppy when they were young, perhaps their first boss was a tyrant. You won't know until you ask them, and they won't share with you until they trust you enough to allow you to help them.

Behaviours always come from somewhere and behaviours can be changed. It's hard to change behaviours of course, but they can be changed. When I talk about saving a vampire. It's not something you can do on your own. There isn't a magic spell you can say or a wand that you can wave. To help someone change their behaviour you need three things. You need patience, you need coaching skill and you need their commitment and belief that they can change. Without the last one, the first two will only get you so far.

To save a vampire means that you are assisting the human to rid themselves of their vampire tendencies and distractions. You are supporting, teaching and helping them be a better version of themselves. You are not controlling the change, you are providing guidance so that they can change.

Michelle T Holland

To slay a vampire means that you are removing the vampire from your life and the lives of those that you are responsible for (eg: if you are a parent, then you are removing the vampire from your and your children's lives, if you are a girlfriend of a vampire then you are removing them from your live and the lives of your friends and family, if you are a manager at work you are removing them from the workplace). Slay does **not** mean kill. Let's be extremely clear about that. If you have kill in mind then put this book down and go find a counsellor to help you rid the vampire that is clearly in control.

Let's discuss the way individuals change to determine when you save and when you slay. As I said earlier, saving should always be where you start, however at some point you need to make a decision about when you should stop saving and get with the slaying.

"Not everyone deserves a place in your life."

You may be thinking that you need to keep saving until the human is saved. This is a sure fire way to remove yourself from your greater purpose, open the door for your own vampire and burn yourself out. Just because you chose to bring someone into your life doesn't mean that they get to stay in it without responsibility. Many people enter our lives and cause us damage. When we hang on to these people for too long we are essentially saying that they are more important than we are. When you constantly keep someone in your life that is toxic and brings negativity into your life then you are allowing your vampire to control you.

Your vampire wants to do all it can to distract you from your greater purpose. Including putting a false purpose in front of you. It will find a 'project' for you to

98

loose yourself in so that you can't achieve your greater life purpose. We all have something in life that we are meant to do, and mostly life is about figuring that out. When we are presented with a person in our life that is taking from us constantly and we struggle to find the good, then we are allowing our vampire to tell us that we are worth less than the other person.

If they are toxic and not adding value to your life, you have tried to save them, and are distracted from your purpose because you are so busy taking care of them, they are a vampire and you need to choose to let them go.

Not everyone deserves a place in your life.

You may be thinking "what if that person is a family member, a sibling on drugs, an alcoholic parent, an abusive teenage child…" well, I have the same advice for you. I'm not going to pretend it's easy letting these people go from your lives, and you may have to do a 'semi-slay' and get some help (see the section on Van Helsing) but you must take action to protect yourself from harm – no matter who the person is that is harming you – you deserve to be happy and healthy as much as they do. You both have a choice. You can choose to remain and therefore you choose the consequences of remaining. If the consequences are terrible you chose them so no complaining. They have a choice to be saved or remain a vampire and they choose the consequence of that. If they stay a vampire and you slay them, then they have chosen that for themselves.

Yes, there is a tonne of complexity, difficulty and emotion that you can wrap this stuff in, but when it comes down to it – you choose the behaviour, you choose the consequence. Here's my obvious disclaimer note - If you believe the behaviour is choosing you (or the person you love) and you are dealing with addiction – get help, get them help, get help for both of you. Addiction is a disease and the vampire will always win without the appropriate help and support.

Let's put addiction aside and talk about the kind of change that you can influence.

Chapter 13: You'll Change the World Kiddo

Don't spend time beating on a wall, hoping to transform it into a door. - Coco Chanel

"You'll change the world kiddo." Said Harry. "But you can't change anyone specifically." Harry and I were talking on the phone after a particularly difficult day for me. As usual I was seeking guidance from Harry, and as usual he provided me with his Yoda style of advice. In the first few years of this kind of seemly incongruent advice from Harry I'd get pissed off and tantrum about not understanding his double speak.

I'd been working with an organisation for a number of months. They were determine to slay the vampires that had taken up residence in their IT department. I was working with the CEO and also the manager of the IT department. They both were saying all the right things, but I knew something was wrong because change wasn't happening as expected. When I was on site change occurred and the CEO and IT manager were very engaged, but when I left for a while to work with other client I'd return to find that they either hadn't progressed or they'd gone backwards. I couldn't seem to get them to change their behaviour so that they could role model the behaviour that they expected in the IT department. I was finding this extremely frustrating so went to Harry for advice.

"How can I change the world, without changing individuals." I said, exasperated. Harry just held the silence and I could hear the smile on his face. "Yes, ok. I know I can't change individuals but I can create an environment where individuals believe that they can change, and they'll change when they want to. I can create the inspiration for change and then hold them accountable for their decision, but I can't change them unless they want to change."

I returned to the business the next day and ask the CEO and the IT manager if they wanted change in their business. They said yes. I asked, are they willing to do the work needed for change. They said yes. Then I asked if they would like me to help them be accountable. They said yes. So I said to them that I expected that they would continue the work while I was away and it was their responsibility to make the changes that they wanted to see. I told them I'd be back in 4 weeks and I set KPIs that I expected them to hit. I was clear that if the KPIs weren't met then I would assume that the change actually wasn't as important as they had said it was and I'd spend less time with them and more with my other clients who were putting in the work to change.

They decided to change and so they did. I spent less and less time with them from that point because they actually did the work that they needed to do to create the change. I didn't change them, I just held them accountable for the decision they made. They did the changing.

You cannot change someone else. I'll say that again slowly because it seems to be something that people get stuck on. You. Cannot. Change. Someone. Else. Actually, it's not even your business to try and change someone else. All you can do is be a good role model, take a supportive role, create an environment where in they can change, help them see the impact of their behaviour and then allow them the time to change. The only way a vampire can be saved, is if they want to be saved. They can change if they put in time and effort to do so. If they are waiting for you to plan the change, make the appointments for the change, and give them the answers then, they are not ready for change.

It's a difficult to save a vampire. Particularly if you are trying to 'change' them. All you can do is provide them with an opportunity to change. They need skills and knowledge, and they need the motivation to change. You can help them find these things, but you can't do it for them. Its not your job to motivate them, its your job to provide the resources and opportunity for motivation and change, but you can't change them without their ok. This is the most fascinating thing when you review the last couple of chapters on the vampire tricks. Even though it appears that the vampire has tricked the human into changing into a vampire or doing their bidding, really the person has chosen the behaviour and action.

I've seen change occur quickly and I've seen change occur slowly. Change occurs the same way humans do everything, individually, stubbornly, and influenced by others. We all have the ability to influence and in the next part I tell you how to engage and influence people broadly. These tips can be applied on an individual basis also. Vampires are masters at manipulation and influence, but they do it for the wrong reasons. Generally, when they are influencing it's for personal gain rather than universal gain. You need to be aware of this when you start to engage with a vampire who has indicated that they want to change.

The want to change is very different from the need to change. We may need to change, ie: we are drinking too much, or we dominate conversations at work, or we are living a destructive life that is not allowing us to live our purpose. We can recognise this and yet we still continue with the behaviour until the desire for change is stronger than the desire to remain the same.

I could write a volume on the way we engage with personal change, but I'll keep it short and too the point because I cover this a lot in volume 1. People change first through a desire to change, secondly through creating a new identity, thirdly through daily actions made on repeat and lastly, accountability. Without these three things being present the person won't change. You can have all the action plans, Apps and spreadsheets you want, but without these elements you will fail.

Let's assume that you are working with a vampire who has the desire to change or a potential slayer that wants to grow their skills. A good process to use to assist them to create an action plan is called the **GROW** method. The grow method is been used for many years by leaders and coaches who want to provide people with a structured process to assist them change. Although I truly believe great change happens organically and through deep inner work, I also know that many people respond to a structured approach in the beginning. Deep inner work may inevitably follow once people start to engage in a structured change process.

The GROW method looks like this:

G stands for: Goal. To have change and to create change, you need to have a goal. You need to have a something a vision in place. You need to have a vision in place that tells you which direction to go in. This needs to be something that you desire. Because if you do not desire a different state then you remain exactly how you are. Setting a goal for change is the absolute first stage.

When you are saving a vampire you need to get them to set their own goals. A mistake that many slayers, managers and other people make is that they set the goal for the other person. You see this time and time again at work and at play,

You have read this book to the end, and so you can spot vampire behaviours. You've read volume 1 so you are a strong and capable slayer. So you say to yourself, "I'm going to save that vampire" and you set off to help them change the vampire tendencies that you spotted. So what you do? You sit with them, you have a conversation with them and then you tell them what you want. Fair enough. That's an appropriate to thing to do.

The problem is when you go the next step and say, and this is how you are going to behave from now on, and this is how you do it. You are super helpful so you write the goal for the person. The goal you've written may be the perfect goal for them and exactly what they need to have an amazing life. The issue is that they didn't choose it. They may not even think that there is a problem in the first place. To set them on the pathway to change, the first thing is to acknowledge there is an issue. Once they acknowledge the problem, and they have a desire to change it, they must take responsibility for it. They will set their own goals.

Sadly, we don't spend enough time working on the acknowledgement and acceptance stage of the change process. Remember I said that once the vampire has decided that they want to change, that they have the desire for change, that's when you implement GROW. Not before. If you try and implement GROW prior to the acceptance stage then you are fighting a losing battle and the vampire will win.

We don't take control of someone else's life for them. They are in control and if they are not in control then nothing will change. It's not your business anyway, work on your own life and your own inner work if you feel the desire to take over someone else's life. You have work to do, because if you didn't you'd know that it is arrogant to impose your will on another and that change will always fail if it's not driven from within.

Just imagined if a friend of yours turned up on your door step. They knocked in your door and came in your house and the first thing that they say to you is "I am really worried about the way you managing your finances." Firstly, I am sure you look at that friend and say its lovely that you care enough to be worried about me. That's very kind of you. The next thing you may think is "What business do they have to walk into your home and tell you that you are not managing your finances?" You may feel very comfortable about your financial situation. It may be different from theirs, but you are happy the way you are.

But that friend continues, because they believe they know better than you (and perhaps they do)…

"I am worried about the way you manage your finances. I am concern that you don't have the skills to manage finances. So, I am going to help you with that. I'm an expert at managing finances and I can tell you exactly how to do it. I'm going to set a goal for you. From today you will save 10% of your income. Every week you are going to deposit 10% of your income into a new savings account."

Sounds reasonable, you may think, and they are just being helpful. I don't necessarily manage my finances that well. I could save more. Is 10% reasonable? I suppose it is, if they say so because they obviously know better than me. I will just go with whatever they say.

But it's not your goal. It's been set for you. How committed are you to that goal? You may be committed to the goal in the first week or so, because you don't want to disappoint your friend. But as soon as something comes up that interests you more, such as that killer set of heels you saw in the window of the department store downtown, you will falter. You will probably also hide your failure from your friend.

Instead picture this. You wake up one morning and say to yourself,

"I am really not doing well with my finances. I really need to make a change. What am I going to do?" You research methods for managing finances and decided the option that works for you in saving more. "I am going to save 10% of everything I earn and I am going to start that this week. I am going to open a new bank account and I am going to start putting 10% of everything I earn into that account. I've determined that 10% reasonable for me."

This is the much more powerful change technique for you. You take ownership for ideas that you come up with yourself. When the idea is someone else's, the ownership is lessened.

You set the goal for you, and they set the goal for them. It's that simple. When the goal is behavioural and you want to help them recognise that the behaviour that they have been engaging in is not helping them, you can introduce them to a behaviour diagnostic tool to help them understand themselves better and what impact their behaviour is having. A tool I regularly introduce my clients to is called the "Lifestyles Inventory" or LSI by a company called Human Synergistics. This tool allows the person to assess their own behaviour style and it has a 360 feedback included so they can assess the impact of their behaviour on others. You can find out more about this tool at www.theslayercodex.com/bookbonus.

If you don't have a goal to aim for, you'll never hit it.

R stands for Reality. Once, we set the goal the next part of the puzzle is assessing what your current state is. We need to understand what's going on right now? And must be real about it. If you are working with a vampire that is showing immortal tendencies then you'll need to explore that with them in an honest way. They must be able to own their current state prior to letting it go and moving into a new state.

Let's say we set ourselves a target to save 10% of everything that we earn. We work hard to it every week. Then sadly one week we lose our job. All of a sudden our financial ability to save 10% of what we earn changes. We may still have the goal of saving, but our current reality says that the goal is going to be difficult at best. Once we analyse our current state and we are honest with ourselves about it, we may need to modify the goal.

When assisting someone to make change, one of the best things you can do for them is help them have a reality check. Many people won't talk about this because they are busy selling you a fairy-tale world where you can have everything that your heart desires. You can wish for it and it will manifest. Now don't get me wrong, I fully believe in the power associated with thinking and if you head to volume one you'll see the 'manifesting' is one of the keys to the Element Yogish. I talk about it differently from

Michelle T Holland

others, but the principle of taking care with your thinking is there.

What I want to be clear about here, is that if you are not real about your goals and your current reality, then you will set yourself up for failure. You may want to exercise for 60 minutes each day, but in reality you only have 20 minutes to spare. Well guess what? 20 minutes is better than nothing so do that. Unfortunately, when people set themselves a goal that is unrealistic they will beat themselves up for not meeting it which distracts them from the change that they are trying to make.

The change they want to make is Goal, and the change they can make right now is Reality. Be real if you cannot save 10% of your income every week then set an appropriate goal for yourself. It can always be modified.

Be real. If you're not real, then your goals never will be.

O is for Opportunity (or Options).
The goal has been set, the reality check is in place. Now it's time to explore what can occur. What opportunities or options are available for change. Your role as a slayer and coach is to help the person to find as many options as possible prior to selecting the one that works for them. Having alternative options allows the person to explore what will work for them now and provided them with stretch goals to work towards. This is useful and helps them stay motivated to the bigger picture.

There are so many opportunities for people to reach their goal, but sometimes they struggle to see them without help. They have to be on the lookout for opportunities. They also have to be open for them. And they have to act for them.

Opportunities are only opportunities if you take action.

Last but not least is W. W is for Will.

Nobody is going to change unless they want to change. I've said this before, but I'll say it again. You can't change someone else.

You of course may be able force people to act in a certain way through threats and coercion, but you can't force them to think in a certain way. Trying to force someone to change is not a trait employed by a slayer. A vampire however won't hesitate to try and force someone to change. But ultimately, it's always the person's prerogative to act or not act.

People have free will. This is a blessing and a curse when it comes to personal change. They can choose to act and they can choose not to. Everyone has a choice and in making that choice they choose the consequences.

So to change, they must have the will and the want to do it. The will is essential because this is the difference between giving up when it gets hard and powering through.

A great Slayer assists the person to discover their goals, reality, where the opportunities are and whether they have the will to make the change. This is how you save a vampire. You help them to save themselves and choose a different way.

To slay a vampire is different. To slay a vampire means that you are taking control of the situation. This is why these should be the last resort.

There are three main ways to slay a vampire. The First way- is to remove them completely from the situation. This may include termination of employment if this is a work place situation. If this is a situation in your home life it may mean you remove contact with this person, either partially or completely. Say no the next time they ask you out for dinner.

The second way that you can slay a vampire is by removing yourself from the situation. They might be your boss, for example, who you can't remove from the workplace. It might be a customer you are dealing on daily basis. You have tried everything to save them and it hasn't helped. In this circumstance, sometimes the best method to manage the situation is to remove yourself from the situation to protect yourself.

I see so many people struggling at work, trying to stick it out. It's not them, that's not working. It's not them, that's not behaving. Yet it is them that are suffering. The place where you go to get money so that you can live your life should not be detrimental to your health, or your enjoyment of life.

I understand the practicality of life. I understand you need a job, you need money to live your life. What I don't understand is for people to stick around when its creating such disappointment and such pain in your life. When you stay in a circumstance like that the vampires have an opportunity to poison you with their toxin.

My advice to you is to protect yourself, protect your health, protect your family. If the circumstances you are working within or living within are so damaging make a decision to do something different in your life. That may come with temporary setbacks, or sacrifices. Don't stay in a circumstance just because you think you should or you are scared of what's on the other side on the door.

Following are methods to enable you to slay the vampires in your life. Take action and reap the rewards.

Michelle T Holland

Vampire Slaying Methods

BLOOD
STORAGE

Michelle T Holland

116

Holy Water:

When you are dealing with vampire behaviour you need to take swift and immediate action. Call the behaviour and ask a question that helps you keep understand why this behaviour is chosen by the vamp and why they believe it's helpful. It's important when calling behaviour and addressing concerns that you do it in a way that assists them to grow. If your action comes from judgement or from your ego then it's best to check that at the door before you speak.

There's nothing worse than a wannabe slayer who thinks they are slaying vampires when actually they are acting like one. Feedback is a gift and the purpose is to help the other to be able to reach their full potential. Judgement gets in the way of this outcome.

Holy Ground:

Remember that time when you were a child and your mum told you that you were being foolish and embarrassed you in front of all your friends? It's awful to have your behaviour or performance called into question, it's worse if it's done in front of people. Sadly we disregard the consequences when we take the easy option and speak about private things in public. Many of you may not realise that when you choose this option you provide a ripe environment for the vampire.

The human brain is a safety seeking missile and when you inadvertently put the person in a position that may appear uncomfortable, their brain will go into protection mode. This means fight or flight. While you believe that you are doing the right thing, the other person's brain has started protecting them by releasing cortisol and adrenaline. These hormones actually impede the memory and reasoning centres of the brain. Addressing concerning behaviours is hard enough without the brain putting up its defence shields.

If you are providing feedback for the other person, then the logical response is to do it in a way in which they are able to respond to it. If you choose to do it another way, then I would start questioning your motivation for providing the feedback. A brief side note for the managers who are reading this. I'm going to be frank with you because I know you can take it. It's your job to give feedback. The reason that you have that job is not to exert your dominance or position, it's to help the other person to learn and grow, and/or determine their fit for the role they are in.

Sun Light:

We look at the world through our own experiences and when we are managing the behaviour or work of another, or dealing with a conflict, we overlay our own personal stuff over the situation and make judgements. They are completely reasonable judgements to us, but may be completely unreasonable to another person. Have you ever been in a situation where half way through an argument you realise that you are actually arguing about the same point. You are both coming at it from your own point of view so it appears that you are saying something different. At some point you sacrifice the relationship for being right about your position.

Getting to know the person will shine light on the situation and you know that vampires can't survive in the light. Understanding their point of view is as easy as asking. Take a break from arguing your point and ask them why they believe that their point of view is serving them. Ask them to explain it to you. Ask them about what value is underpinning their point. You will discover that knowing the persons values and why they believe what they believe will help you to address the situation. You may never agree with it, but you'll come to a more reasonable position. Decisions made in anger and judgement are often the wrong decisions.

Synthetic Blood:

Whether you want to save a vampire or slay, you need to give them the opportunity to change. Before the change happens there needs to be a few things out in place. You need to set expectations about how you need them to behave and when you expect to see change. By setting times to follow up and discuss progress provides accountability.

It may appear like the behaviour change is not real to begin but sometimes compulsory compliance is needed prior to voluntary compliance being implemented. If you are clear in your expectations, you hold them accountable for their actions and you support the change by allowing it to happen you'll have more chance of saving. If they are still damaging your relationship or your work outcomes and you've tried hard to save, then you may choose to slay.

Don't Invite Them in:

It's important to understand any personal issues that may be present before launching into saving or slaying because it helps you to determine the most

119

Michelle T Holland

appropriate course of action. Be careful not to take on their personal issues. Too often I see slayers taking on the problems of the vampire. They get bogged down with the personal issues which distracts them away from addressing the situation appropriately. As soon as you take on someone else's problem as your own you stop them from having a voice and stop them from being the hero of their own life. You want to be there to support them as much as you can and you want to be able to create an environment which can facilitate change. What you need to be careful of is appearing and taking control of someone else's life like it is your own.

There's a lot of good intention wrapped in unintentional arrogance. You want to save the day for the other person and essentially tell them that you are better at life than them. You may be better at your life but no one is better at someone else's life. Just remember that the person you are dealing with is fighting a vampire and you can help them, but you can't do it for them. Focus on your responsibility and allow them to sort out their own lives.

The Stake:

What is at stake? What is happening that means that the vampire is surfacing? And what is your part of the mess? Understanding and acknowledging your part of the mess is all part of the process and no matter how much we'd like to avoid it, we can't. Many times when I speak with people about understanding their part of the mess I get push back. This is because we like to do the blame game and push our responsibility away. It's not a judgement or criticism it just is what it is. We are human first and foremost and as a human we want to stay safe and protect ourselves. We put ourselves at risk when we take ownership of mistakes and the parts of us that aren't perfect.

To help someone else to fight off their vampire, or to remove a vampire from our own lives we have to get real with the part we play in the situation. We need to do this so that we have the full story and we are able to come to the correct course of action. We also need to do this so that we can empathise with the human who is trapped in the vampire's clutches. If you can't empathise (ie: I've been where you are and I've felt what you feel) and you can't see where you have a part to play in the relationship, then it will be difficult for them to 'hear' what you are saying. If you look like you are perfect and have never faltered, then they may reject your interventions.

Re-souling:

This step is simple to state, and often difficult to implement. Once a human has taken charge and is working hard to change, you have to give them opportunity to make the change, and to make the mistakes that come with working at change. It's too easy to tell someone to change and then have an expectation that they just will. But if you have ever tried to change a behavioural aspect of yourself you will know how hard it is.

Take removing sugar from your life. I know many people who swear by taking the sugar out of their diet and they get so many benefit. And I also know how difficult it was for them to remove the sugar permanently. They made a commitment to change and a promise to themselves (you know that's the first step from The Slayer

Codex Volume 1), and then they set about making the change. They start eating more protein and vegetables. They drink more water, and they remove the processes sugar from their days. However, then a stressful event happens and they immediately reach for the chocolate bar. They know it's not good for them, and they know the benefits of a sugar free life so why does this happen? It happens because we are human and therefore fallible, and fall victim to our internal vampire. There's no problem with this. The problem comes from what happens next. Generally what happens is the human starts beating themselves up for choosing the chocolate and they may even decide that they've 'ruined it all now' and go also for the piece of cake and the glass of coke. Now they feel like they've really blown it and head back into daily sugar land. This is when the vampire has once again taken hold and has found the gap in the armour. If we don't allow ourselves to acknowledge that change happens because of the mistakes and slip ups them we don't allow ourselves to change, and we certainly don't allow others to change.

Be careful of what is call the theory of confirmation. This is where our brains seek out events and behaviour that 'confirms' what we already know to be true. This is the big bungy cord of change initiatives. We move towards the change we want, but there is this identity that we continue to hold onto and as soon as we (or others) make a mistake that identity is confirmed and 'boing' we start back at the beginning again.

Be aware that people are going to make mistakes, they are going to boing back to the beginning, and we are going to seek out the behaviour that confirms their previous identity. So being tolerant all around is the order of the day.

Van Helsing:

In volume one I shared my how to find a GURU. Go back and refresh on that chapter if you get to this step. Get help from an expert may be necessary when helping a human to tackle their vampire. People you generally call on when you are working are human resource officers, supervisors, managers, business or life coach, legal advice, or financial advisor. If you feel like you need help then don't be afraid to ask for it, particularly when you are dealing with something outside of your comfort zone. Just be aware of the person you are asking help from because some people's advice helps and other's hinder. Well-meaning people are just that, well-meaning, but it doesn't mean that they are an expert or have the right answer for your situation. There's a great quote that says "If you think it's expensive to hire a professional, wait until you hire an amateur."

There are times when you will be dealing with your own vampires, or helping others, and you'll recognise that your skills have reached the end of their usefulness. It's not because you are deficient in anyway, it's just because some situations require a more specialised skill set. Many people continue to deal with deep issues from their past and they may require a person qualified to understand them and help them work through them before they can manage their vampire.

There was a reason that Mina and Jonathon passed on their Dracula problem to Van Helsing. Don't be afraid

Michelle T Holland

to bring in your own expert and hand over to someone qualified where you are not

It's Time to Slay:

"If you can't change the person; change the person." This was a quote said to me by a senior human resource executive many years ago when we were talking about coaching managers to be better managers and leaders. Although a simplistic way of talking about behaviour change, and vampire infestation, it rings true in many ways. There will be times when, after all effort is given, that the person refuses to give up their vampire and they need to be slayed. Just be very aware and clear that you cannot, under any circumstances, change a person without their say so. Change happens from within. Terrible circumstances aside, we are the creators of our own destinies and you have no right to think you are able to control someone's change nor the right to engage in trying to control their change.

Saying that, you may need to make a decision and request that they leave your life or leave your organisation (where you are a manager responsible for the person). The decision is obviously yours, but it has occurred because the other has chosen not to leave, therefore it may appear that you are 'taking' their choice away. You are not. You are acting in the best interest of yourself, them and the organisation (if this is a factor).

If you have done everything you are able, to help the person to reclaim their life from the vampire and they still remain unwilling to change, you need to slay. This may be terminating employment if you are a manager at work, it may mean leaving a toxic relationship, or it may mean removing a specific behaviour you hold through psychological intervention.

PS: "slay" if you haven't realised by now is code for removing the toxic behaviour (and person in some cases) from your life and the life of the people you are responsible for - I'm not talking about killing or hurting someone. I'll be super clear, so that I'm not misconstrued in any way. In no way, no how, and at no time ever, do I ever support, or tolerate, violence as a method for managing conflict.

Closing the Coffin:

After a particularly long battle with a vampire a slayer friend of mind confided that she was struggling to let go. She kept seeing the vampire behaviour in others around her, she questioned what she knew to be true about the vampire, she questioned her slayer skills, and she was not allowing herself to move on. She knew that it wasn't helpful for her and also that it was affecting her health, but she found it hard to let go. I was concerned for her because I know that when we don't allow the vampires to fully leave our lives and our thoughts we are at risk of our own vampire taking hold. She had been in a particularly toxic relationship with a man who was abusive and it took time and courage for her to remove him from her life. The problem was, although he physically wasn't there any longer, she was still carrying him around with her in her head.

After we spoke about how she was feeling and we debriefed on how she handled the vampire slaying, she worked up additional courage and went to a therapist to sort through the left over thoughts in her head.

Michelle T Holland

It's important to take time to debrief on a slay. This is because we can blame ourselves and question whether we did the right thing. In my experience it appears that this happens more for female slayers than male slayers, but I have no evidence to site. Regardless of gender it's an important part of the slayer process to debrief. There are two key outcomes that you will get from debriefing:

1. you will feel supported by the person you are debriefing with and can celebrate the action that you took to remove a vampire from your life; and

2. you can learn from the situation and determine if there were areas where you could have handled it better.

Both outcomes help you be a better slayer in the future.

So the moral of the story is, when you save a vampire rejoice because it's a feat that many people are unable to achieve, and also take the time to close the lid after you slay or you may be doomed to repeat the mistakes of the vampire or allow your vampire to take over. Slaying and saving vampires is not a simple task, and you won't get it right every time, but following this process will assist you to do it in the best possible way.

Part 4: Get Others to Help You

The quality of a leader cannot be judged by the answers he [she] gives, but by the questions he [she] asks.

- Simon Sinek

Michelle T Holland

Unearthing Vampires

Can I tell you the real reason that I started writing down The Slayer Codex? I hope you said yes. The main reason is because I made a promise. I made a promise to Harry when he first revealed the secrets of the vampire and how to unleash my slayer. I promised him that when I could I would pass on everything I learned from him and from my own experiences as a vampire slayer. Through my travels I trained people, I coached and I mentored. I worked with organisations and I worked with individuals. I've lived that promise over and over. However I didn't feel like what I was doing was enough. I could continue to work one on one and with businesses, but I could only reach a small number of people myself.

I started to look for ways that I could get the message out without compromising my integrity. I knew that I could continue to run training and ask my slayers to pass on their learning as Harry had asked me, but I knew that they would be learning and growing their own skills and it would take time for them to feel comfortable to pass the knowledge on to others. I wanted to reach more and more people and give them the original message. I had embedded so much of my experiences, successes and failures into this methodology and felt I was under valuing it by sharing it within the limits of my work.

A colleague said that I could start speaking at conferences and events. This appealed to me, however I knew that a great deal of my success in dealing with vampires, and in particular helping people to release their slayer, was to do with my anonymity and to speak publically would dissipate that advantage. So after much deliberation and thought I decided that writing down the Slayer methodology into a book would be the best way to get my message out broadly while protecting my anonymity.

It was a great plan and I spent a year writing the first Slayer codex. Quickly I discovered that just writing the damn thing wasn't enough. It took fricken ages to write it and then sat on my computer waiting for the right people to come along and discover it. I thought that there would be a massive rush of people wanting the secrets that I had. There wasn't the stampede of potential slayers beating on my door that I expected.

I knew that there were potential Slayers out there because I've met many of them through my journey but trying to find the others I hadn't met yet became a challenge. What I learnt is that the people who you want to follow your vision are not just waiting around for you to fall onto their Facebook feed or into their office. They are busy living their own lives and they have their own distracting 'stuff' going on. They are probably even thinking that you are a burden putting more pressure on them.

This is where I started to learn about building a community of like minded people. I spoke with my guru and he helped me to understand that people will only follow you when you have something to offer that they want. It sounds like a 'no-brainer' but we all get so focused on how awesome we think our idea is we forget that the person on the receiving end may not have the same passion for it as we do.

So I learnt how to influence and how to engage. My guru gave me a book called "Tribes" by this dude who is obviously a Slayer, Seth Godin. The book was an eye opener for me and helped me understand how I could get people to firstly hear my message through all the noise and then to love my message enough to become Slayers themselves.

I read many more books that told me that I needed to engage and influence. I found online mentors and YouTube clips that told me that 'becoming an online sensation' would make me rich and help me spread my message, but not many gave me the 'how' I could do that in a real way. So I read everything I could get my hands on, asked lots of questions, and through experimenting I figured out that I needed to engage and understand the person that I wanted to talk to first.

You need to engage and influence people to get your message heard. There are changes to be made and without people on board, they just won't happen. I'm not going to bother telling you all the reasons that you need to engage or tell you that you should engage. You're smart enough to figure that out yourself. What I'm going to give you here my friend is how you figure people out so you can engage them.

Michelle T Holland

Chapter 14 – Talking to Slayers and Vampires

> *The single biggest problem with communication is the illusion that is has taken place. – George Bernard Shaw*

Communication can be a bitch. It is hard to get it right and its essential for engagement so you must learn how to do it as well as you can or you will be unable to influence the people you need to influence. It's something that every people asks for more of, and yet it's something that many people are either not great at, or they take it for granted that it actually happens. There are so many distractions in life and we busy ourselves with them to the point where communication becomes something that we add to our check lists. We send an email or a newsletter and believe that we have communicated.

Michelle T Holland

"Communication is a 50/50 pursuit and you are 100% responsible for your 50."

You are 100% responsible for your part of the communication which means that if your audience doesn't understand what you are saying then you may be doing something that is contributing to them being confused. If they are confused, you may be confusing. If they are bored, you may be boring. If they are not interested....well you get the gist. It's essential to do your part of communication well.

What I see too often is people communicating in a way that makes sense to them, but they are not focused on the audience. Let me be really blunt, people aren't interested in you or your stuff, unless it has a direct impact on them.

WIIFM (what's in it for me) is a common acronym bandy about in office buildings or on sales training, but many people are still determined to ignore this basic communication principle. I see too many people get on their high horse and say that people 'should' just understand that the thing they are talking about has a greater purpose and will create success for the business. Well, if you can't describe how it affects that person directly then they won't buy what you're selling, it's as simple as that. Whether you believe what you say is going to save the world, no one else cares, unless it's going to impact them. You must acknowledge this in your communication and get down from the high horse, or you will experience a big fall when your horse bucks you off.

If you are truly interested in communicating and having your message heard by the people who need to hear it, then you need to communicate in a way where they can.

There are a few things you can do to make sure that your communication is going to be influential and have impact. If you can tick off the following items in your communication then you will start to engage the people that you want to engage. You will find more slayers who will share in your passion and purpose, and you will have better luck in convincing vampires to change their ways if you can speak directly to them with influence.

Here are 5 tips to make your communication more influential and more engaging for slayers, vampires and humans:

Tip 1... Make it Relevant and Tantalising

What is the most pressing issue for you right now? What is keeping you awake at 2 am? What is the topic you discuss most with your significant other or friends? I'm guessing that it didn't take long for you to recall the issue that you are dealing with right now - whether it is a positive or negative issue is of no concern. The point that I'm illustrating here is that your problem is way more important to you than anything I'm dealing with.

Even if you are the most giving and empathetic person on earth you still are more consumed by your own life and issues than anyone else's. If you are consumed by someone else's life then generally you are focused on how it is consuming YOU. You may not want to hear this, or you may want to argue, and that's your choice, but the fact of the matter is – humans are concerned with themselves first and foremost. Therefore to be able to communicate with them you need to focus on what's in it for them. Let me address the question that may be playing in your head right now.

"What about people who are interested in saving the world more than their own self. They recycle, they donate money, they go to rallies, they work in homeless shelters, they change the world. What about people like Gandhi, you can't tell me he was interested in himself more than others." Stand with hands on hips, chin raised. "So there."

First let me address the 'Gandhi defence'. We still talk about Gandhi and the events that he undertook to change the world seventy years after they occurred because there haven't been many other Gandhi's since. Other than Mother Teresa, who apparently gave selflessly also, try and think of ten people like Gandhi, ten people that selflessly give their life, their livelihood, and their health to further a cause. Its ok, I'll wait.

I'm hoping that you came up with at least one or two more people out of the billions of people who have lived on this planet in the last seventy years. Billions of people who have had the same opportunity to make the same impact as Gandhi, and yet most of us would struggle to name ten. This is because he is unique. His achievements extraordinary.

In 1913 before he returned to India to take on the Brits, Gandhi led a campaign of civil disobedience against the South African government. He was disgusted by the treatment of Indian immigrants by the South African government. He was successful and the campaign changed the tax and marriage laws that restricted Indian immigrant's civil liberties. This was an amazing feat and he must be commended. The other thing that happened in 1913 was the passing of the Natives Land Act in South Africa which essentially locked the native South Africans off their lands. They could no longer lease farm land from Europeans, and it stopped them from having businesses or owning land in South Africa. This act essentially kicked off the times of Apartheid which held strong until the early 1990s. This law allowed atrocities and injustices that denied civil liberties from another group of people in South Africa but Gandhi didn't fight for this one. Now don't get me wrong, I absolutely applaud the achievements of Gandhi and that his actions essentially introduced the world to a non-violent way of creating change, and I don't believe he is responsible for changing everything that is wrong in the world. The education and principles of his actions are his legacy. But to draw this back to what I was saying about people not caring about anything outside of their own interests, he could have engaged in the same campaign for the native South Africans also. He chose to fight for Indian immigrants because it directly affected him, he was an Indian immigrant so it was personal. This doesn't diminish his impact on the world, on the contrary, it further demonstrates to me the power of getting your message right for the right audience. No matter where the motivation comes from, when you do it right, you can impact the world.

As much as I love talking about the great leaders of our time, let's get back to understanding communication and how you can get your message out, and become one of those great leaders.

To have an impact, and simply to be heard, your message must be relevant to the people that need to hear it or they'll switch off and find something else that's interesting. To make it relevant for them, try to discover what they are interested in. For example, if you sell teeth whitening products, only people interested in whitening their teeth will listen to your message if you talk only about teeth whitening. However, many people are interested in presenting a confident and polished image to the world. So if you are selling teeth whitening talk about the benefits of teeth whitening, higher self-confidence, self-image, professional look, etc. If they are interested in having a professional image and whitening their teeth will help them with that, then you've got them interested in having a conversation about your product.

Think about it like this. Your perfect audience member is watching TV and they have access to 1000s of channels. They flick through the stations until something grabs them. If they are a travel buff then when their brain sees a show that looks like travel they will stop. If they're are interested in teeth whitening, then an info commercial on white teeth will get them to stop. If it's interesting, relevant and/or novel, then they will remain watching. If it's boring, they'll continue on their flicking journey.

This is communication. If you aren't presenting something that makes them stop they'll just flick to the next channel. Once you have them you need to present the information in a way that is interesting or tantalising.

There is a reason that we find gossip so hard to resist. Our brains are hard wired to find information and actions that confirm what we already know to be true. We are social beings so gossip provides us with a low investment social interaction. This is also why social media has become so prevalent in our current daily activities. We like to see what others are up to and particularly if its juicy, but we don't want to spend too much of our limited time and energy doing it.

I know though personal testing that if I put a post on Facebook that leaves the reader wondering about a situation then I get much more engagement than if I just put the whole story. Cryptic is not good and just seeks to piss people off, but tantalising is great. You give them just enough to wet their appetite so that they want to know more.

So when communicating the trick is to be relevant to the audience (side note - not everything you have to say will be relevant to everyone so don't get disheartened), and you need to be tantalising.

Tip 2... Sometimes the truth is enough

There are times when communicating is difficult, to say the least...actually communication appears to be difficult most of the time! These are the times when telling the truth is often enough.

You may find yourself in situations where what you need to communicate might be perceived negatively or unfavourably. There might be redundancies in your company due to economic down turns or you may have to tell your loved one that they didn't hang out the laundry the right way...

Whatever the communication method generally the advice that I give is, sometimes the truth is enough.

Michelle T Holland

However, to be honest without upsetting someone takes skill. Here are a few things that you can do to ensure communication is honest without harm.

- **Be clear and concise.** Make sure your message and your expectations are completely understandable.

- **Start with the end in mind.** Make sure when you communicate, you do so to accomplish a goal.

- **Don't procrastinate on bad news.** Don't wait until you think the time is right. A very smart person said to me once, "It will never, never, never, not ever, be the RIGHT time." Always communicate the truth behind the bad news and explain what's going to happen next.

- **Speak in simple language.** Steer clear of jargon, corporate speak and slang. Talk to your audience as if you are speaking with a smart 12 year old. It would be a shame to hide your message behind turgidities so to appear grandiloquent.

- **Prepare and practise.** Prepare what you're going to say and practise. Make sure that it is completely understandable with actions to take away. However, when you do communicate, do it from the heart.

- **Just the facts mam.** Have all information and proof available. Be as specific as possible in relating the facts. Make sure you use concrete examples to support your position.

By communicating the truth, you stand a better chance of weathering any type of bad news with your reputation intact. Be direct and honest, and the people you are communicating with will appreciate you for it.

Tip 3… Be an Authority

Authority is one of those words, like aggressive, or conflict, or power, that we sometimes assign a negative overtone. I think this is because when you look at the definition of authority you see 'the power or right to give orders', and we associate 'orders' with a boss or manager that we don't like. We associate this with a feeling of inadequacy or submission. When you dig in further into authority what it also means is someone that knows what they are talking about. A person who has gained knowledge and wisdom though

experience.   You are an authority in your speciality area   whatever that is.

"Influence: The Science of Persuasion" by Robert Cialdini gives us clear insights about how people listen to and respond to a person of authority.   They conducted studies to prove that people are more likely to follow, listen to or buy from someone that they believe is an authority. Funnily enough authority comes from a feeling of confidence in the person not necessarily the traditional way we see authority (ie: he's the boss/she's the manager etc).

You can build your authority by adding value for people and being confident. Now confidence is a huge big subject and probably a whole volume of codex on its own. There are many ways you can start to build confidence but basically it's all a matter of mindset. Did you know that you can influence your feelings of confidence through your body language? Anne Cuddy, author of the book Presence has conducted a great deal of research and has shown that standing or sitting in 'power poses' (think of Wonder Woman – who I love – standing strong hands on hips) increase yourself image and confidence. It's a great book for developing a great awareness of your presence and how your posture can affect your behaviour.

Pull your shoulders back, lift your head up high, believe in your abilities and 'be' confident.   You'll eventually start to feel confidence when you continue to act this way.

Other ways to show authority without looking like a jerk is to demonstrate your competence and keep current in your field. If you can talk about the most recent research

Unearthing Vampires

and findings in your field then you will be seen as an authority by others.

Tip 4... Using Social Proof To Build Trust

This is where I tell you that humans are sheep. Well, actually I should probably explain in a much nicer way but that's the colloquial version.

Generally, no one wants to be the one to go first. We sit back at school, in University, or at a meeting looking at the others to see who's going to be the brave one to speak first. Did you know that only about 2% of the population are entrepreneurs, wealthy or innovators? This means that 98% of us are sitting waiting for someone else to take a leap first to test the waters before we wade in. This is not a problem, it's just life. We need the innovators to drive society forward and create new things. Think 'Apple' and Steve Jobs for an easy and obvious definition.

However, the next wave of people after the 'innovators' are also really important. They are called the 'early adopters' and make up about 13.5% of the population. These are the ones that bought the Macintosh Computer and the very first iPhone. They are the ones that bought the first DVD player even though their VCR worked perfectly fine and the DVD player was $2500. These are the trend setters and these are the people that most marketers want to get on their side because then marketing become a breeze through word of mouth.

Saying that most of us are in the middle of the pack, i.e.: early and late majority (at about 68%). This is because of that 'brain as a safety device' thing I've spoken about before. We want to make sure that someone else has ironed out the kinks before we spend our own money,

143

Michelle T Holland

time or emotional energy. So we wait for the leaders to
toot it and then tell us about it and then we'll get on board.
We're sheep. Again not judging just observing.

This is important to know when you are developing
your communication message. You are more likely to be
listened to by the majority of people if you have some
proof that someone else has tested what you are saying
than if you are telling them something brand new and
untested. Remember that only about 13% of your
audience will listen if its brand new and untested.

So when crafting your message ensure that you have
an element of social proof in there. This can be in the form
of statistics.

*"67% people surveyed said that this thing I'm saying
is really important to them and their family".*

Or it can be in the form of testimonials from clients or
endorsements from someone important:

*"That thing that she is saying is amazing and it totally
helped me out." Signed Someone*

Or it can be in the form of case studies:

*"Here is Jen, she did the thing I'm talking about and
now look at her."*

This also works well one on one, not just in group
messages. So if you are working with a vampire or a slayer
and trying to convince them that what you are doing is

important, don't just tell them, use social proof to show them.

Tip 5... Understanding their Head Space

Understanding the way others think is like opening a magical portal into a world that you didn't know existed. Once you can truly get into the head space of someone you are talking to and understand where they are coming from your communication will become a breeze.

I once worked with an organisation that had invested a lot of money in sales training. They had a minor vampire so asked me to come and work with them. At first they told me they were a bit sceptical about the amount of money that they had invested previously on training, and couldn't understand how a 'profiling' survey could really help them with their vampire or their sales, two important outcomes from their investment.

Following the workshop and after getting their profiles. They started to figure out how they could get more sales by really understanding the thinking style of their clients. They put new actions into place and were amazed at the results. I called the CEO about 2 months after the workshop to see how they were going and he was amazed at the insight he'd gained just through doing this simple tool.

"It's like witchcraft. I feel like I'm able to predict what the other person is going to say before they say it. And not because I'm judging based on who I am but instead because I've made an assessment of what profile I think they may be primarily. I then adjust my communication to appeal to them. Sales galore and its only been a few weeks!"

Michelle T Holland

He's the type of manager and client that every Slayer wants to work with. He learns and then he puts it into practice. He was also willing to admit that the investment was worth it for the people who implemented.

That is such a good point and a side note. If you are going to invest time and money in learning something…put it into practice immediately. If you don't then you'll lose the skill and waste the money.

So what was this magic that he spoke of? Well it was a simple profiling tool that helps people examine the way that they think. To do the full profile and have coaching is the absolute best way of learning, but I'm going to go through the basics here with you as a start. The profile that I recommend is Hermann Brain Dominance Indicator (HBDI or WholeBrain Thinking) which examines your thinking style in depth. You can find out more at www.theSlayercodex.com/bookbonuses.

When you are communicating with someone you will start to notice a pattern. If you are savvy and can ascertain their thinking style then you can start to understand their motivations and therefore where their natural energy comes from.

Each of us get our energy from a different place. I'm not talking about the energy that we get from food, I'm talking about the energy that comes from within. The energy that your inner Slayer releases to you when you are stimulated by something that you are passionate about.

Understanding the other person's motivation is a start towards understanding what they believe their purpose is. This has two benefits, one you can communicate with them on a level that gets their interest and also you can help them discover their purpose and inner Slayer if they haven't found it already.

Sadly, most people wander through life without a broad sense of purpose or passion. They tend to be primarily motivated by their own personal short-term interests. They will sit idle on the couch waiting for something to happen.

Without allowing their Slayer to be released they will find that their energy and motivation is depleted no matter what food they eat, how much coffee they drink, or how much sleep they get.

True sustainable perpetual energy comes from discovering your purpose and taping into your passions. Your Slayer is your energy source. By focusing on understanding the other person that you are working with or trying to communicate with, then you will have more luck helping them unleash their Slayer and conquering their vampire.

A final tip for getting better at communication...

Ask. Yep, if you want to know the best way to communicate with someone, or you want to know something about the other person you are working with, just ask them. I know it's a surprising and novel concept.

Michelle T Holland

You would be amazed at how many times someone has said to me, "I just don't know what they were thinking?" Or "I don't know where their head is at?" Or a statement like that. Can you guess the answer that I provide… ASK THEM!

We spend so much of our time making assumptions about others instead of just asking them. So how do you ask? You just do. Come from a compassionate and curious mindset and speak to them from your heart. If you really don't understand what that were thinking, ask them.

Warning: when asking a question its best to ask in a non-judgemental way for a better response. Asking "*WHAT* were you thinking?" is going to inflame the conversation and the other person will not respond well. Ask instead "Can you tell me what you thought about when you made the decision and why you choose that direction to head?" It'll get the answer that you really need.

Becoming a master communicator is going to be one of your best weapons in the fight against vampires.

Chapter 15: What Happens Next?

*Here's my hunch: nobody's secure,
and nobody feels like she completely
belongs. Those insecurities are just
job hazards of being human. But
some people dance anyway, and
those people have more fun. —
Glennon Doyle Melton, Carry On,
Warrior: Thoughts on Life Unarmed*

You are now armed with a tonne of information about how to firstly unleash your slayer and ignite your inner light, and secondly to identify vampires and deal with them. So what do you do with all of that information?

Well isn't that just the million dollar question?

I can't give you the answer to that question, because the next part of this puzzle is for you to make a choice about what you do next. Some people will put this book down and never think about it again. Some people will put the book down and start thinking about how they can implement it in their life and determine its too much like hard work. Others may start implementing some of the elements and may start seeing vampires around and that's where they leave it.

Each of these choices is valid for that person and their current stage of development. This book isn't for everyone. Even many of your friends who you think are ready for this book may not respond to it the same as you have. Don't let that deter you from placing this book in their hands. Remember my story about "Eat, Pray, Love"? Even if they read part of it now and put it down, they may pick it back up in the future and change their life. They won't have that opportunity to do this if you don't give the book to them in the first place.

So where to from here for you? If you haven't read volume one, then I encourage you to pick it up and read it. You will find that it helps you to manage the vampires in your life more than you would expect. By understanding and strengthening your inner slayer and resilience then you will be more likely to be successful in life and business.

I haven't spoken a lot about the outcomes that you can expect as a result of doing the work needed to become a fully-fledged slayer who is lit up from the inside. I've briefly spoken about the wellbeing outcomes you can expect, but I didn't cover the financial, personal, business and social outcomes. I generally resist talking about them because for me the journey of becoming a slayer has been the greatest outcome of my life and the success that I've had as a results has just been the cream on top. You will discover your own version of success through this process and when you feel that your slayer has become a part of who you are, you'll know you are successful.

The other reason that I often avoid talking about these successes is because people have a tendency to compare their beginning with another's middle or end. This leads to a feeling of inadequacy which I don't want for you. Comparing which leads to you feeling bad about yourself is not worthwhile, and is the work of the vampire, not the slayer. Compare only to give yourself a benchmark to work towards and recognise that everyone's individual success is as a result of hard work and failures that you may not see immediately.

I recognise that everyone is at a different part of the journey and some of you may need a little more motivation, and if so that perfectly ok. So I'm going to briefly talk now about the success outcomes that are typical of this kind of work.

Obviously, we're not going to be silly and believe that everything on this list will magically happen to us because we've read the book, right? These results are typical when you put the effort in and do the work associated with the elements of the slayer methodology and the effort to save or slay the vampires in your life. If you choose not to do the work, on a consistent basis, then you can't expect to get the same results as slayers who have put in the work.

Michelle T Holland

Slayers that put in the hard work can reasonably expect outcomes such as;

- Feeling a sense of wellbeing and gratitude;
- Experiencing a great sense of self-esteem;
- Realise their full potential and are recognised for their strengths;
- A higher level of personal wellbeing and wellness (ie: you get sick less);
- People want to be your friend and work with you;
- Regularly are issued the cool projects at work;
- Have closer relationships, and work harder at maintaining good ones;
- Have less toxic relationships and people in their live;
- Are more likely to receive payrises, and career promotions;
- Have greater success in business due to their ability to engage more fully with their clients;
- Increase their wealth as they attract abundance into their life;
- Are more likely to be sought out by others to provide assistance or guidance;
- Improve their ability to take in and retain knowledge; and
- Have less stress related injuries and illness.

These are results that I have personally experienced, and have seen in the clients that I work with. They are also backed up by countless studies conducted, many of which I've touched on during volume one and two.

When you reduce stress in your life, you increase your self-image, you become self-actualised and you work hard at the outcomes that matter, you will discover that you experience many if not all of the outcomes I've named above.

The journey to unleashing and strengthening your slayer and taking action to manage the vampires in your life is one that you cannot retreat from once you start. Although at times you will feel exhausted and want to quit, the benefits to your life and your future will be worth the hard work.

If you don't work, your dreams won't either.

Good luck on your journey, I know that you will love being a slayer.

If you are curious about what it would be like to have a skilled slayer as a mentor to help you through this journey and become more of the person you are meant to be then please visit www.theslayercodex.com/bookbonuses where you can access resources and specials reserved only for those who invest their time and energy into reading The SLAYER Codex.

All the best for your journey.

Michelle T Holland

Resources

If you want to take back your life, you need support. Resources can be found at theslayercodex.com and SynergyIQ.com.au.

We look forward to helping you slay the vampires of your life.

Michelle T Holland

About the Author

Michelle is an author, entrepreneur, coach and business consultant.

Leveraging her interest in people and business development, she traded in her accounting career to pursue her undergraduate and graduate degrees in human behaviour, organisational development and ethics. Having held a range of positions in human resources and senior management, Michelle is proud of her successes. Among other accomplishments, she is particularly proud of the leadership programs, workforce planning methodologies, and business transformation strategies that she has created and implemented.

In 2013, Michelle started a boutique business consultancy (SynergyIQ) where she specialises in leadership development, change leadership, business improvement, and culture transformation. In 2016, along with her partner Pete Barter, she developed an online platform that is revolutionizing the music education sector. The platform manages administration functions so the educator can focus on teaching and finding new clients, through the system.

Throughout her career, Michelle has worked with many organisations including Anglicare, ShineSA, RenewalSA, SA Water, AHPRA, Novatech Creative

Michelle T Holland

Event Technology, the City of Charles Sturt, the City of Salisbury, City of Greater Bendigo, Helping Hand Aged Care, the University of South Australia, the National Trust of SA, Meals on Wheels, and BusinessSA to name a few.

As a keynote and guest speaker, she has spoken at conferences and live events across Australia. Her speaking topics include leadership, business culture, resilience, and personal leadership branding.

An accredited leadership coach and culture profiler, Michelle's professional associations include Human Synergystics, Hermann International (HBDI), Australian Human Resource Institute (AHRI), the South Australia Writers Centre, and the Leaders Institute of South Australia. Michelle also volunteers as a mentor for young entrepreneurs and young business professionals.

She has travelled and worked throughout Australia, Canada, the United States, England, Scotland, France, the United Arab Emirates, Egypt, Jordan, Malaysia, Thailand, Borneo, Singapore, Bali, Fiji, and New Caledonia.

Michelle T Holland is the author of 'Culture Inc', 'Energy Vampires Suck', and 'Unearthing Vampires', and lives in South Australia, with her two children, her partner, two adorable dogs…and a cheeky rabbit.

Conference Speaker

Keynotes, masterclasses, and engaging presentations.

Michelle is a member of the new generation of speakers and authors who give generously to their audience and maintain relevance through continual research and development. Each presentation is a bit different, because as Michelle learns and grows, so does her ability to provide a unique look at the world through the creative and curious eyes of a corporate problem solver. Michelle enables her audiences to think creatively and act differently to create better businesses.

She will provide your audience with information, resources and direction that enables them to lead a transformation either within their business, or themselves. Her favourite topics are business effectiveness, transformational leadership, and leading culture transformation.

"Michelle is personable and approachable and a pleasure to work with. She found time for all the delegates that approached her for further information at the event. I cannot recommend her enough. The expertise she brought to the event was invaluable to everyone in attendance!"
Doug Power, Event Manager IQPC

Michelle T Holland

"Our participants left Michelle's presentation with a renewed sense of energy which was fantastic given it was the after lunch session! I'm pleased to recommend Michelle as a spear who engages and educates."
Taryn Sexton, CEO LG Professionals

Find out more about Michelle at
www.michelletholland.com

Michelle's other books

Energy Vampires Suck is available online at Amazon or www.theslayercodex.com

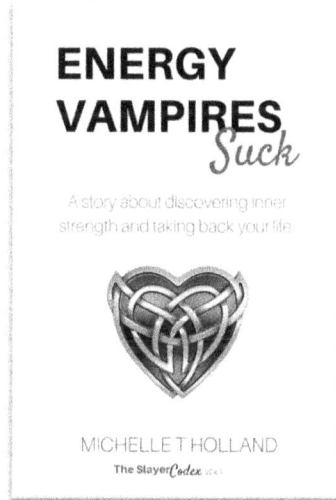

ENERGY VAMPIRES *Suck*

A story about discovering inner strength and taking back your life

MICHELLE T HOLLAND
The Slayer*Codex*

Culture Inc is available online at Amazon or www.synergyiq.com.au or in good bookstores.

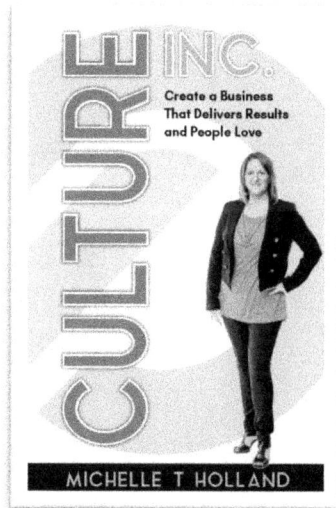

CULTURE INC.
Create a Business That Delivers Results and People Love

MICHELLE T HOLLAND

www.ingramcontent.com/pod-product-compliance
Lightning Source LLC
Chambersburg PA
CBHW061724020426
42331CB00006B/1084